Family Matters and More

Stories of My Life in Soviet Russia

by

Sol Tetelbaum

PublishAmerica
Baltimore

First printing

ISBN: 1-4241-7087-7
PUBLISHED BY PUBLISHAMERICA, LLLP
www.publishamerica.com
Baltimore

Printed in the United States of America

Dedicated to the memory of my dear parents
Dvoira and David Tetelbaum

Acknowledgments

These recollections were inspired by our family's dear friends, the late Dorothy and Joseph Friedman. They were our volunteers, the people who helped us to adapt to our new life in America. The stories impressed them and they became the great enthusiasts who encouraged me to write the memoir.

It was not an easy task to write these stories, because they don't constitute a translation. They are an attempt to tell Russian stories in English and at the same time retaining the author's genuine way of expressing himself.

This writing could never be done without the considerable help of many people. First of all there was the help of my wife Susanna, my son Vladimir (Vova) and my daughter-in-law Alicia. Their help was crucial; they corrected everything with great understanding and care, not wishing to change the "Russian flavor" of my writings.

Two more people I would like to especially mention. They are my friends and first readers: a retired college counselor Art Naftaly and an English teacher, Marlene Wilson. These five have done the most difficult and most sophisticated work, sacrificing an enormous amount of their time checking the manuscript. I am grateful to all of them—their contribution is impossible to overemphasize. Marlene and Art supported every step of my writing and inspired me, not letting me to drown in my numerous doubts.

I also would like to thank Eamonn McKay and Nelly McFeely, who also were among my first English-speaking readers and supporters. Eamonn's thoughtful comments related to the first part of the manuscript were very encouraging and helped me a lot in my writing.

I thank Eric Rosenblum for his candid criticism that was very useful and gave me interesting ideas for improvements of my writing.

I thank my granddaughter Suzie Smelyansky, who impressed me with her remarkable grasp of my writing.

I am grateful to my daughter Dina and my brother Ruven (Roma) for their support and for refreshing my memory about some family events.

I thank all my friends and my readers for their constant support and encouragement.

Contents

Introduction

Let me please introduce myself. I am a former nuclear research engineer and college teacher who was born and lived almost half a century in Odessa. During my life in Odessa, I experienced a lot, but in good times and in bad times, there is nothing better for the true Odessian than a good joke. And before starting my life stories, I would like to tell my readers a short story that based on an Odessian anecdote about the first Odessian immigrants in America.

Aunt Betya and her family were among the first who emigrated from Odessa directly to America. Very soon, she considered herself as enjoying the full rights of being an American. The whole world knows that all Americans are rich. And what do rich people usually do? They send presents to their "less rich" friends. Aunt Betya felt the necessity to do the same. It was supposed to prove that she was a real American.

The family had just come to the country. They didn't have money, and all adult members of the family were looking for jobs; however, that didn't stop Aunt Betya—she knew what to do. Saving some money from her shopping, she went to the closest Thrifty store, selected, according to her judgment, some things she thought best, and sent a parcel to her former neighbor and friend, Aunt Dusya.

When Aunt Dusya received the parcel, she didn't open it immediately. She decided to wait a little until she could call all her neighbors to look at the nice things she had gotten from America. But rumors were ahead of her. All the neighbors rushed to gather long before Aunt Dusya had a chance to inform each of them personally.

When, surrounded by neighbors, Aunt Dusya opened the parcel, she found sneakers, a pair of jeans, a couple of T-shirts, a plastic electronic watch, and then one more thing which evoked an energetic discussion among the neighbors. The mysterious thing had a size of approximately fifteen to eighteen inches and had an egg-shaped, rather oval form with turned-down edges. Its outside surface had rug-like red fiber.

"What is it?" exclaimed Aunt Dusya.

"Don't you know?" said neighbor Masha. "It is a decorative pillow cover." She recently got married and knew everything related to bed and bedroom decorations.

"So if it is a pillow cover, why does it only have one side?" said Masha's old grandma. "I know what it is. It is a rug for feet which people use to put on the floor near their beds to protect feet from cold."

"Then, why it is so small?" asked neighbor Misha. "I am sure it is a pad for a car seat." Misha was an auto mechanic and considered himself as the best expert in the car field.

"But cars have two seats," neighbor Anton disagreed. He remembered his sad experience when once car seat springs badly harmed his buttocks.

"It is only for the driver's seat; driver should be protected first," insisted auto-mechanic Misha.

"You are all wrong," Aunt Dusya decided to enter into the discussion. She really was a smart old lady. "I know what it is. It is a kind of a cap, it is a beret," and she tried to put the thing on her head. But the thing appeared to be too large. "Well," said Aunt Dusya, still not giving in, "it is a beret for a big person," and she passed "the beret" to her neighbor, Anna. Anna wasn't a very large person, but had a big, horse-like head. "Try it," ordered Aunt Dusya. Neighbor Anna tried the beret, and her head hid under it up to her neck.

The next day, Aunt Dusya sent a thank-you letter to her friend Betya. In the letter she wrote: "Dear Betya, many thanks for sending me such nice presents. Everything is great. By the way, the beret you have sent me is beautiful, but, unfortunately, it is a little too large."

In her reply letter Aunt Betya wrote: "Dear Dusya, I am happy that you liked the things I have sent you. To tell the truth, I don't recall sending you a beret, but if you need one, let me know, I'll try to find it.

As I remember, I sent you sneakers, T-shirts, jeans, watch, and a toilet seat cover. I don't remember sending you anything else. What beret are you talking about? Many kisses, your friend, Betya."

I have to say that far from everything that happened in my life could be told with the same humor, but I hope that the readers will appreciate the humor of this funny story and it will be helpful to read about events when no remedy existed or a joke was the only painkiller.

Preface

At the end of the eighties my whole family, which included my wife Susanna, daughter Dina and son Vova, son-in-law Igor, and granddaughter Suzie, immigrated to the United States where life in many aspects is totally different from life in the Soviet Russia. I lived in Soviet Russia for over fifty years. Many things happened to me during that time; I witnessed many big and small events, both political and personal.

Life is attractive by its diversity, and more often we remember things which are of interest to us. There are events and occasions in the life of every person and every family that, for one reason or another, remain in their memories for a lifetime. These things can also be of interest to many other people as well despite their personal nature. Knowledge about such events enriches our own experiences and deepens our understanding of life; they make us think about things we have never thought about before. It is especially attention grabbing and frequently can be educational to learn about personal lives of people from different countries. Apparently, these thoughts were also in the minds of my first readers when they recommended that I publish these stories.

In these recollections, I limited myself to some stories that, with a few exceptions express my thoughts and feelings related to personal and family matters and not burdened by politics, ideology, etc. Of course, the political situation in the country badly affected the life of each Soviet family, including ours, but the political and social issues that occurred during my life, and my working career and its difficulties, are a different topic that requires a separate writing and a different approach. However, relating what I write here will give some insight to what it's like to live in the Soviet Union.

The stories I have described reflect many sides of our lives, and because of this they are different: hilarious and serious, dramatic and tragic, merry and sad, philosophical and worldly. Some bring laughter; some bring tears.

Not all of the events are equal in their significance; nevertheless, they are all worthy of telling. What these stories have in common is that they all are true, all of them to a greater or lesser extent made an impression on me and are engraved in my memory. With minor exceptions, all of the stories are narrated in chronological order. I hope that the reader will enjoy them and will be able to compare, at least partially, life in the Soviet Union with life in America.

I wrote mainly about my human family, but I think it shouldn't surprise the reader to find out in this book that several pages are about our pet dog, also a loyal member of our family.

Any personal story has a priceless value for understanding life of an older generation and connections between generations. Unfortunately, such stories have been rarely published. I love my parents; nevertheless, I know a little about their lives. I regret not being sufficiently insistent in asking them questions in order to know more about them and our origins. Therefore, I was unable to include as much as I would have liked to about them. There was only one story which was told by my father and which has left an impression on me since childhood. I will start my reminiscences with that story.

This book is true stories about my life in the Soviet Union. Describing these stories, I have identified some people, both relatives and non-relatives, leaving real names for family members, some relatives, and myself. Names of some non-relatives have been changed.

One

A Loaf of Bread

Before my emigration, for over fifty years I lived in Soviet Russia where the shortage of food was as habitual as the government's promises of forthcoming paradisiacal life for all the Soviet people. Now I live in America, in the country where people are fighting with obesity and doctors strongly recommend limiting fat and bread consumption. This is a wise advice, but I eat my meal to the last crumb and sometimes, seeing how I am picking up every tiny bit of bread, people cast a strange glance at me. (Though, gradually, I am loosing this habit.)

No, I am not hungry for food; it is just my habit that I developed in my home country where traditionally bread is one of the most important things. It symbolizes life, prosperity and good will. It is an ancient Russian custom that people meet the dearest guests with bread and salt, and they kiss bread as a sign of the greatest respect.

As a child, I did not care about food and could not understand why, according to Russian manners, it was impolite, even a sin, to leave something on the dish or bite a slice of bread and leave it uneaten. Then I heard a story about an incident which happened to my father and which changed my eating habits forever. Many years have passed since I heard the story, but it is still in my memory.

It was Soviet Russia in the early thirties. There was havoc and breakdown everywhere. After the October Revolution in 1917, the Soviet authorities made the land state property. They also forced all farmers to pay so-called food taxes with grain. Because of the severe shortage of food and extremely high taxes, farmers often paid food taxes with seed grain which they saved for future crop. After several years of such policy and bad harvests, the country turned into a huge island of starvation. Every year hundreds of thousands of people starved to death. Bread remained the main and sometimes the only food that was possible to buy, though the price was astronomical. Except for the food, everything else lost any value.

It took a long time before my father's family saved enough money to buy a two-pound loaf of rye bread. After counting and recounting the money over and over again, Father rushed to the local market. Coming to the market, he saw a neatly dressed gray-haired man, who was selling several loafs of rye bread.

The bargain was long and hard. At last, Father bought a loaf, but in addition to the money, the seller demanded the watch he saw on my father's wrist. It was the only watch Father had, but it no longer mattered to him: An empty stomach doesn't need to know time. Father held the loaf like a priceless crystal bowl. It seemed pretty heavy. "Maybe I have lost my strength, or maybe I have already forgotten the weight of bread," he thought.

When he came home, the whole family discussed how to divide the bread. They decided to cut the loaf into seven pieces, a piece a day, just to spread the pleasure for a week. Then Father tried to cut the loaf and couldn't. The knife didn't go through. When finally he managed to break the loaf open, what he saw made his stomach shrink so painfully, as if somebody poured acid into it. The loaf was filled with rusty nails...

Two

Siberian School

1941 to 1948

I was born in Odessa, a Ukrainian city on the Black Sea. When the war with Germany began, my family was evacuated to Siberia. At that time I was five; my brother was twelve. My memory retained a little about my early childhood: bombing, evacuation, killing cold weather, my endless pneumonias, and the unimaginable long way to Siberia where we were going to live.

Finally, we came to our destination point, the city of Cheremkhovo. It was a remote East Siberian town with small and old coalmines. The region had a fair coal-bed, and some of the mines still worked, providing many Cheremkhovo citizens with employment. But some of the mines were so old that they no longer contained any coal, so the authorities closed them down.

When we arrived in Cheremkhovo I was seriously ill. It was pneumonia (the fourth or fifth case in a short period of time), and my mother gave way to despair. Because of my countless cases of pneumonia, colds, and lack of food, I became weak. The doctor who saw me and gave me a thorough examination by tapping and listening through his stethoscope, concluded, with sympathy in his voice, that the situation was hopeless. We had no money or other real valuables that could help provide us with quality food. Almost everything we had we left in Odessa. I don't know how it was possible but, at the last moment, Mother grabbed a small Persian rug to take with us, and she exchanged this rug for a special food that would help me survive.

There were no accessible drugs available for the treatment of pneumonia in the USSR, and doctors usually treated it with aspirin. Just before the war broke out, a new and much more powerful drug called "Sulfidin" (Sulfanilamide) appeared in Russia. For the ordinary people, there was no way of getting their hands on the medicine. It was only great luck that for several pre-war years my mother worked for the medical department of the Railroad Transportation Administration. The department helped its people to escape the German occupation. Just before the evacuation started, they received a few doses of Sulfidin, and they gave one single dose of this new medication to my mother, just in case of emergency, because she was a department employee who had two small children. Mother saved that single dose, and when I became ill, she divided the powder into six or eight small parts and gave them to me. I don't know whether those small portions of drug played any significant role or whether it was Mother's ceaseless devotion, but, as she later said (and she sincerely believed in this), a miracle had happened and I survived.

We lived in Siberia for seven years, and for the first several years I felt the consequences of my bouts with pneumonia. I experienced some problems with my health, and for this reason I spent every one of my summer vacations in the so-called TB resorts for children with weak lungs. All such resorts were located in Siberian pine forests, which were well known for their excellent pine air. Because of the constant lack of food and the never-ceasing feeling of hunger, the forests had some additional advantages: we could always find some edible plants, roots, berries, etc. However, it wasn't always safe. A couple of times I picked up something, ate it, and poisoned myself. Fortunately, the poisonings were not life threatening and ended only with vomiting and diarrhea. After that I became more cautious and followed all our caregivers' instructions.

I began my school years in Cheremkhovo. The school was conveniently located not far from the barracks, and I remembered it as a big two-storied building with a large hall, large classrooms and wide stairways. In my memory, the schoolyard where we played was like a football field.

I never thought that I would see the school again, but, much later, maybe after thirty or thirty-five years, I got a chance to refresh my memory, and it turned out to be an interesting experience. It was the late seventies or early eighties, when I was working for the Odessa Polytechnic Institute. I went on a business trip to the city of Irkutsk, for a presentation at a scientific conference. The distance between Irkutsk and Cheremkhovo was approximately sixty miles or so, which meant about two, maybe two-and-a-half hours of traveling by train. When we lived in Cheremkhovo, two trains ran between Cheremkhovo and Irkutsk. One (the morning train) the people called "Worker"; the second one they called "Collective Farmer" ("Kolkhoznik").

Many people lived in Cheremkhovo and worked in Irkutsk. The city was one of the oldest in Siberia and an administrative center for the Irkutsk region. It was also the largest city in the region. Working as a chief bookkeeper, my father had regular business trips to Irkutsk, and sometimes he took me along with him. Visiting Irkutsk was a new and wonderful experience for me, and two things I remember stroke my memory the most. The first was that instead of muddy Cheremkhovo roads I saw streets paved with short wooden logs and wooden sidewalks; and the second memory was the sweet and sparkling carbonated water, which wasn't available in our small town, and which I asked my father to buy me wherever I saw it.

So, being in Irkutsk on a business trip, I reserved my one free day to visit Cheremkhovo. I wandered on dirty city streets and could not recognize any of them. The city authorities had renamed almost all streets. I went to the city educational department and explained to one of their employees what I was looking for. She told me that the school had been closed down, and showed me how to find it. I spent over an hour looking for it, and when I eventually found the school I had a hard time recognizing it. It was an abandoned two-story small wooden building with a tiny schoolyard. I remembered the location of my classroom on the second floor, and when I found it, I could not believe that almost thirty students could fit into it.

I attended the school for five years, until we left the town. It was an ordinary school, and while the teacher taught us during school hours, after school there was nobody to look after us. We played military games, jumped from roofs, exercised on horizontal bars, and did many other boyish things. We swam in the summer time and skated a lot during the winter. In the fourth grade, I found out that I liked drawing and I drew what I saw around me. I began to attend art classes for the beginners organized by one young amateur teacher. After running for several months, the school discontinued the classes because of a lack of paper, pencils, and other basic supplies.

Although we were in elementary school, some of us liked to watch the physics experiments that our physics teacher performed for older students. He had a large closet room where he kept his experimental paraphernalia. Nobody ever guarded the school or the closet room, and nobody cared to lock it securely. That was until the day that tragedy struck.

Two boys, both of whom liked to watch the physicist's experiments, broke into the school late in the evening and broke the small hanging lock on the closet door without much effort. They discovered an alcohol lamp and a small vessel filled with mercury and decided to see what would happen when mercury boiled. Although mercury never boiled, the experiment ended tragically: during the school meeting the teacher told us that one of the boys was severely poisoned and died. I mention this tragic accident because my friends and I were interested in such experiments as well, and any one of us could have been with the boys.

Three

Crime Dramas

1942 to 1946

When we lived in Cheremkhovo I was a small boy, and being preoccupied by my own kid's business, I don't remember too many details of the life of adults. I do remember how we moved to a new place to live.

Our new apartment was actually a room in a box-like house called a barrack. One long corridor divided the box into two symmetrical parts, each of which had several rooms with doors to the corridor. Two identical barracks were built next to ours. A couple of funny comic-dramatic episodes that happened while we lived in the barrack are still in my memory.

Cheremkhovo was a village-like, small mineworker town. There were drunks everywhere, mostly men, and if they could get their hands on pure alcohol, they would drink it undiluted. The atmosphere of war which brought to the surface many criminals, made all newcomers feel unsafe.

Our family occupied one room in the barrack. A couple of older people occupied other room in the same barrack. The walls of the rooms were wooden, and sounds in one room could be heard in almost any other room. It was common every evening for people to lock all their doors, and nobody let you in without being assured of who you were.

One late evening, a drunken man from the neighborhood confused the barracks and tried to get into room where the couple lived. Unaware of who he was, the old women asked suspiciously, "Who is this?" The intruder mooed something, like a hungry bull, but failed to identify himself. He continued dully knocking at the door, trying to open it. Scared to death the woman and her husband desperately looked for a place to hide.

When the knocking became more insistent and threatening, the terrified husband took a rake, which they used for the furnace, and began hitting an iron frying pan crying, "Where is my rifle? Give me the rifle, I am going to shoot the rascal!" After a couple of minutes, the whole barrack was buzzing like a disturbed hive—the conference took place without anyone daring to leave their rooms. Finally, someone did leave the room and showed the unwanted visitor his way home.

The second "crime drama" happened in our barrack as well. It was the day after a holiday, and I was standing in the corridor waiting for my playmate who lived in the same barrack. There was a single common toilet for all the residents of the barrack, located at the very end of the building, near the common kitchen.

That day, I saw a neighbor enter the restroom, and just a split second later I saw him jumping back out as if scalded. At the beginning, I didn't pay much attention, but when I saw a second man, then a woman repeating almost identical pirouettes my curiosity lit up. I approached the toilet, opened the door and looked inside with great interest. I was disappointed: there was nothing inside except used crumpled pieces of newspapers on the floor. Some more pieces of newspapers were hanging on the nail hammered in the toilet wall. What was so scary there? I understood nothing.

Later, the next day, I overheard my parents talking and learned what happened in the toilet. We had no luxuries such as toilet paper, and almost all of us used newspapers for the purpose. Somebody brought in a holiday newspaper with pictures of Stalin and other Soviet leaders printed on it, and used it as toilet paper. At that time it was an unthinkable crime which could have cost someone his life. And the toilet visitors, seeing decorated pictures of Stalin and other "people's favorites" were scared to death that they could be suspected, but nobody knew what to do. At night one of brave barrack residents took care of it. When my parents saw me listening to them with great interest, they told me to keep my mouth shut. I was smart enough to understand what that meant.

One more drama in our lives in Cheremkhovo has been engraved on my memory. It happened shortly after the victory in World War II. Unexpectedly, we received a letter, forwarded to us by the International Red Cross. The letter was from somebody of our relatives, who emigrated from Russia long ago. They were searching for us.

The letter was short: "Darlings, Dears, where are you? Are all of you alive? Please respond; let us know about you. Such an awful war smashed our lives, and we don't know whether you are alive or not. Please, we beg you to respond to us." Together with the letter we found a photo of a baby girl. It was a picture of their daughter.

My parents read the letter with fear: in the Soviet Union, it was dangerous, almost a crime, to have relatives abroad; such family connections could have cost my parents their freedom, or even worse. Thinking that I wouldn't understand what was going on or wouldn't pay much attention, my father absentmindedly discussed with my mother what to do with the letter. I overheard their discussion. They decided that they would destroy it, although they did save the photo.

Four

The Dream Called a Bicycle

1943 to 1948

Usually our lives weren't notable for events, but sometimes something unexpected could happen. Once in my life I became rich, very rich, and it happened almost overnight, although my way to that lucky day was quite lengthy. My happiness didn't last long, but it is a different story.

We, children of the war, had few joys in our lives. Most of the toys and things we played with we used to make ourselves. But some things we weren't able to make and couldn't afford. We dreamed about them, hoping for gifts or miracles to happen. Like everyone else, I had my own dream. The dream was called a bicycle, a real, two-wheel bicycle with a leather saddle, shiny frame, headlight at the front, and air pump at the side. This is what I wished for most, and I have to add that at that time it was an extremely expensive wish. I realized that nobody was going to give me such a gift.

The dream was just a dream, but life had already made me a realist, and I didn't have much hope for miracles—I began to save up money. It was easy to say: "to save up." During the war, money almost lost its entire value; food and goods became extremely expensive, and on top of this, during the occupation, the Germans flooded the country with false paper money. Money became nothing more than worthless paper, and people preferred "natural" exchange (bartering): food for goods and goods for food. However, the government still paid salaries in cash. Because the salaries were ridiculously low, and the very basics could easily cost a month's salary, people tried to buy everything from the local stores because their prices were much more affordable than market ones.

My parents used to give me a little money for food and small things, and when I decided to buy a bicycle, I spent as little of my slim "allowance" as I possibly could. However, most of my savings were coming from my parents, relatives, gifts from other people, and generous money came to me on my birthdays and some Jewish holidays.

Only a few of my elderly relatives dared observing Jewish holidays, and I didn't know much about the traditions. I didn't know the history of those holidays and dates, but one holiday I remembered pretty well and eagerly waited for it. Of course, it was Hanukkah. Adults called money presents "Hanukkah-gelt," the word "gelt" being Jewish-Yiddish word meaning money. Hanukah was a real celebration for me: I was the youngest in our "Mishpukhah" (the circle of relatives in Yiddish), and all the adults gave me generous money gifts. Initially I kept my money in a tin, but then I had made another important step toward my dream, albeit an unusual one in the circumstances: I opened an account in the local saving bank.

Why was it so unusual? Well, the fact was that not many people kept money in the saving banks, especially during the war. First, people had no extra money; they could hardly make ends meet as it was. Secondly, those who did have money, and sometimes it was a lot, preferred to keep it hidden at home because usually most of it was made illegally from speculations, black market manipulations, or other similar illegal business practices. Understandably, these "businessmen" didn't trust the government. Most importantly, they were afraid to keep the money in banks. How was one supposed to answer the immediate authorities' question: "Where did this money come from?" It was an open secret that few people could legally make significant amounts of money. The Soviet government liked better to reward people for their hard work with nice words or diplomas instead of paying them. My friend when somebody thanked him for something usually said, "Oh, 'thank you' is too much, ruble would be enough." People who had extra money preferred to keep it "under mattresses," in hidden places, or somewhere else. So, the banks weren't too overcrowded.

Visiting the savings bank I felt like an adult, like an important person. A teller gave me a standard bank saving book where the bank kept records of my deposits, withdrawals, and balances with the tellers' signatures. I burst with pride: Just think, an eight-year-old fellow was coming to the bank to do financial business, sign forms, or make deposits. Another factor that warmed me up was the thought that should I have wished, I could have taken money from my own account without asking anybody's permission. Frequently, I would go to the bank to deposit even the smallest amounts of money—maybe three rubles, maybe five. The bank tellers knew me; they liked to see me in their bank and treated me with warmth. I felt that I brought a little bit of life, some fun, or, at least, something new into their boring working days.

During my years of "financial activity," I managed to save up a fair amount. After years of stringent saving, I was ready to buy a bicycle, and maybe even something else. I was waiting for the time when my long-awaited dream would be available in the local store, or when I would get a chance to go with my father to Irkutsk, a big city where it was possible to buy a bicycle.

Then, one day in 1947, rumors spread across the town that the government was planning to do something with the money, but nobody knew for sure what the rumors meant, or when the planned changes would take place. When my "star day" came, I learned that the government replaced the old money with new at an exchange rate of ten for one. It was "devaluation," and it meant that all money became worth a tenth of its previous value. There was a small exception which made me rich. For those who kept their money in the banks, the first 3,000 rubles didn't lose value at all. The next 2,000 lost only twenty percent, and only the rest lost ninety percent of its value. Thus, my several thousands almost didn't lose value. It was as though I had several tens of thousand of the old money.

On the day when the money was devalued, I saw lines of people at the saving banks; all carrying bags full of the old paper money to exchange. To avoid suspicion and trouble many people made their exchanges in small portions, going several times to different banks. The great irony was that sometimes the bags themselves had more value than the money they contained.

Looking at the people with bags, I thought that it was my great luck that I kept my money in a bank; it actually helped me to become rich overnight. I felt like I was an American "tycoon," and it made me happy and proud. I was sure that I had seized my dream by the tail, but, alas, my happiness didn't last long.

My parents knew everything about my personal account. They encouraged me to keep the money in the bank, and to make my life easier they sometimes gave me some extra rubles. Soon after the devaluation, Mom told me, "Sonny, I am sorry, but we badly need this money for living. We will buy you a bicycle later." Being kids of war, we were frequently nasty and selfish; nevertheless, we clearly understood what "money for living" meant. It was awfully hard and frustrating, but I gave all my money to my parents.

When we returned to Odessa I still wished, occasionally, for a bicycle, but I no longer tried to save money. What is the point of becoming rich if you can't reach your dream? When I grew older, it became too late to buy a bicycle and learn how to ride. So, unlike many of my friends, I have never learned how to ride a bicycle. Besides, other wishes replaced my "bicycle" dream.

Five

Lesson of Surviving

1943 to 1944

Our parents worked day and night and we had more freedom than we could safely handle. Though we were normal and healthy kids, many of our games were too risky, maybe even dangerous. We just could not comprehend their danger or, like all kids, did not care much about our safety. The arms and ammunition we played with were handmade toys, but the wounds were frequently pretty real. A couple of serious "gunshot" accidents ended in visits to the hospital. In the summer, tired from our wars, we liked to have a rest on a river.

There were two so-called rivers in the town. The first one, which ran through the town, was tiny and incredibly dirty. It was more of a creek with muddy, stinky water and a lot of garbage and other stuff both on the surface and on the bottom. The name of the river was "Cheremshanka," however, people just called it "The Stunk" (or the Stinker). Adults avoided coming close to its banks, but we did not care much about the water purity or our health, and so we swam and dived in its poisoned, filthy waters. It was a miracle that we had no serious health problems and were not killed.

The second river, called Oka, flowed several miles from the town. The reader should not confuse it with the big river Oka that runs into the river Volga. This Siberian Oka was much smaller than its namesake, nevertheless, bigger and cleaner than Cheremshanka. It had beaches, places for swimming and recreational areas where some owners kept their fishing boats. Our Oka was the river in which I received my unforgettable swimming lessons.

When I was seven or eight years old, our adult neighbors took me with them to go fishing. They had a big boat, more of a cabin cruiser, with a wide deck and a small cabin. The day was uncommonly sunny and hot; the boat was floating in the middle of the river, and we were resting on the deck enjoying such a rare opportunity.

One of the men on the boat asked me, "Can you swim?" I could not, and actually feared deep waters, but when my "coach-volunteer" offered me a swimming lesson I gladly agreed. He smirked, then approached me, and, without hesitating, pushed me into the water. It happened so unexpectedly that I did not even try to paddle, and because I was swallowing water, I sank to the bottom like a stone. The man waited for a while, making sure that I had swallowed enough water, then he followed me in and pulled me back to the deck. When he repeated his lesson for the second time I showed considerable progress by beginning to fiercely beat the water with my hands even before I sank. Alas, the result was the same: I went to the bottom, and he rescued me again. I desperately resisted him when he tried to push me into the water a third time, but my struggle was in vain. I was scared, and everyone just stood around watching this spectacle, and laughing. After the third or fourth time, to everyone's surprise, I was somehow able to keep myself afloat for a couple of minutes. By then my teacher-tormentor had decided that he had taught me my lesson, and so left me alone.

Over sixty years have passed since then, and although I don't remember the faces of my "coaches," I still vividly recall their swimming lessons. When I look back on my family's emigration, I am reminded of those swimming lessons. For us, new to that adventure and unsure of what lay ahead, it was a case of sink or swim.

Six

The Good Deal

Although in all maps and documents, Cheremkhovo proudly called itself a city, I would rather call it a big village. Probably, that wouldn't be fair either: Cheremkhovo differed from a village and the difference wasn't negligible. First of all, the city had a mining industry; secondly, and maybe, more importantly, it had a big city market. Indeed, Cheremkhovo's market, as I remember it, could make a city from any village.

The market was located almost in the center of the city and was enclosed with a wooden fence which was almost totally broken down because of its old age and the severe Siberian climate. However, the fence still existed in the minds of drunkards and cows. Drunkards usually lay in places where the fence was before (they considered it "under the fence"), and at the end of the day the cows, returning home from their pasture, habitually went around the market as if the fence still existed.

The market, as any self-respectful market, had a large plaza where the second-hand goods market (in Russian slang called "Barakholka") was located. Still, some area inside the plaza was available for tour performances. The Barakholka was not only a goods market, like a specific superstore where one could buy everything necessary (more frequently everything unnecessary), but also a kind of cultural center-museum. Moreover, museums commonly didn't have things which one could see in the Barakholka. For this reason: Cheremkhovo "intellectuals" liked the market and often visited it to buy or just to look at "exhibits."

My relative, older than me, a kind and reasonable young man, he was one of the more frequent Barakholka visitors, and the subject of his interests differed with some peculiarity: he liked bargaining. It became his passion. Not because he wanted to buy something—he liked the process of bargaining itself. Usually, seeing some interesting thing or object, he asked its price and then he gave his offer that was so much lower than the asking price that once he was nearly beaten for his humiliatingly low offer. In some cases, when he felt that the seller was almost ready to give up, he changed his mind, found something wrong with the thing, or found some other reason not to buy it. He had a huge experience in bargaining, but he had never bought a thing. He managed to keep that tradition up to a day which some of my older relatives could remember.

Initially, that day wasn't different from any others. The young man wandered along the market looking for something interesting, until he came across an unusual "exhibit." It was a pocket watch with a big odd case reminiscent of a Soviet alarm clock that showed the right time no more than twice a day. The seller, a guy with rotten teeth and foxy eyes, who looked like a criminal asserted to potential buyers that it was a Swiss watch. Seeing a potential buyer approaching, the seller rubbed the watch by his sleeve and put it in his pocket.

The excitement of the hunt awakened something in the man. "Why are you hiding it?" he wondered. "Let me take a look at it." And keeping the watch he asked, "How much do you want?"

The guy said, "It is a Swiss watch, look what the inscription says. It is foreign letters; I can't read them," and took the watch back.

"You keep it upside down; let me take a look at it," the buyer said and again took the watch. Keeping the watch, he continued, "Are you selling it or what? How much?"

The seller said, "I see you are an expert, as for you, my lowest price would be..." and said the number.

"What?" the young man was flying into a rage. "The golden watch costs less," he said.

The guy didn't want to give up. "It is a priceless watch; can't you see it? How much would you pay?"

Nothing could restrain the purchase hunter. The guy was small and slim, and the young man wasn't scared that the guy would beat him, but instinctively pressing his head into his shoulders, he offered the price a hundred times lower than the seller wanted. The seller's reaction was immediate: "Good. It is yours. Where is the money?" he said. There was no way back.

The young man brought the watch home and the next day showed it to a watchmaker. The watchmaker glanced at the watch and his verdict was short: "Shit," he said and turned away. For a long time the watch traveled from one place to another, absorbing dust and becoming covered with stains; finally, it was given to me.

I used all my imagination, but couldn't think of what to do with it. Then I separated the case from the mechanism and used the case for mixing watercolors.

The purchase had an unexpected effect: although he won, but since then, the young man never visited the market again. He lost his interest in bargaining. Too easy victory is humiliating for the fighters. Besides, he wasn't sure who won.

Seven

Curiosity Killed the Cat

The Cheremkhovo market was like an entertainment center for us, the boys who lived not far away from it. However, arriving at the market, we weren't free to do what we wanted. We had bosses. Several older teenager-hooligans ran the show. They divided the market into "spheres of influence," and were "supreme rulers" within their "sphere," and enforced there the "Jungle Law." For safety reasons, all younger boys were forced to look for the protection of self-assigned "rulers."

I used to come with two boys, older than me. I called them "Shkalik" and "Nose" ("Shkalik" is Russian slang for an eight-ounce bottle of vodka). Our "protector" was a teenager, seventeen or a little older, whom behind his back I called "Fiksa"(Russian slang, means a metallic tooth crown)— he broke his tooth in fighting with other "bosses."

Usually Cheremkhovo wasn't spoiled with visitors, but sometimes, actors on tour visited our town, and it was a real holiday for many townspeople and especially for our gangs. One such "holiday" became most memorable for me. Unexpected visitors brought a one-day show, called "New Attraction." Nobody knew what did it mean. The advertisement on the wall of the main market building promised that everybody would be able to communicate with souls of dead people.

When we learned the news, we became extremely excited and rushed to the market. Each of us was eager to know what it was all about, but nobody could tell us, except that the visitors looked like Gypsies. Rumors, one more ridiculous than another, circulated everywhere. On top of that, impatient Fiksa pushed us to learn details.

We went to search for information. It wasn't difficult to find the place where the show was supposed to be. We were idling around, watching how three Gypsy-looking bearded men constructed a tent, long like a corridor.

Nose brought the rumor that bearded performers were going to hide the souls of dead people in the tent. Of course, we wanted to check the rumor, but the men didn't let us look inside. That ignited our curiosity even more.

Soon, in the early afternoon, the tent was ready. Like hunters, we waited for the men to leave the tent, so we would have a chance to get into it. To our great disappointment, the bearded men didn't leave the place. We surrounded the tent and were ready to take it by storm. Our "enemies" guessed our intention. I heard as one of the men said to other one, "...anyway we are going to start soon." After a short whispered discussion between them, one of the bearded men, slyly smiling, suggested that we be the first visitors of the attraction. It wasn't a free lunch. They required us to pay and to do it immediately and then all of us should "get lost."

Only Fiksa had money to pay for the show. He also was able to loan the necessary amount to Nose. Shkalik and I rushed to Shkalik's uncle who was a shoemaker and worked in the market. Borrowing money we returned very soon and saw how Nose popped out from the tent exit. Fiksa stayed not far away from the tent exit watching around. He was gloomy, his lips shook, but seeing how Nose flew from the tent and his perplexed face, he began laughing, mixing laugh with foul words. Seeing us he abruptly stopped laughing and, using his "delicate" slang, explained to Shkalik and to me how delighted he was with the attraction and how "f... great" was what he and Nose saw inside the tent. I began suspecting something and wanted to ask him if he saw the souls, but the bearded man called for the next visitor. There was no time for questions and we ran to the other end of the tent entrance. Shkalik entered first; I was told to wait.

After a short while, they told me to enter. I paid for the permission to enter and entered in the tent. Ink-black darkness surrounded me. The funereal voice from somewhere inside ordered me to move. I slowly felt my way. A hidden record player began to play a funeral march. Suddenly somebody grabbed the collar of my shirt and pulled me somewhere. The collar squeezed my throat, making me hard to breathe. I was horrified and began to resist fiercely. The grasp came loose, and at the same moment I felt a strong kick below my waist and like a bullet, I flew into darkness. My head went through the tent and with force hit Nose in the stomach. The foul words poured from him as corn from a torn bag and Fiksa again began to laugh hysterically. The show was over; my fanny was aching. Apparently communication with souls was too strong.

One of the bearded men approached us. He was smiling from ear to ear and his face shone like varnished boot. He offered Fiksa and Nose cigarettes and said, "Have you communicated with all the dead souls you wanted? Not all? Well, come later. If you keep your mouths shut I'll treat you with wine and herring." (Siberians called vodka a wine).

My mother didn't let me go there for the second time. She said that it was too late. The same night the attraction with all "communicators" disappeared. I was sorry, I wondered to see others "communicating" with the "dead" souls. Although all communicators asserted that the show was impressive, nobody wanted to go into details. Everybody kept their mouths shut, and me too, even though I wasn't expecting "wine with herring." I had gotten a valuable experience, and since then, when people say, "curiosity killed the cat," I know exactly what they mean.

Eight

Back to Odessa

1948 to 1953

In 1947 I received my first graduation certificate from the fourth grade of Cheremkhovo elementary school, and a year later, after fifth grade, in the summer of 1948, our family left Siberia and moved back to Odessa.

My parents already knew that German bombers had destroyed our home. A bomb hit the apartment building where we were living before the war, and most of the destruction was on the third floor where our apartment was located. Many apartments, including ours, which we shared with our relatives, were looted—everything was gone.

So, for the first several months after our return, one of our relatives gave us a shelter, and we shared rooms with her. Her tiny two-room apartment was on the second floor of the old, half-ruined two-storied house which had no facilities. The house had a rectangular form with a small yard in the middle of the rectangle where, near the back entrance stairway, a dirty and stinky public house toilet stood. Such conditions were typical not only for postwar Odessa but for almost all cities in the country. Besides our family of four, four more people shared the same apartment with us.

When we came to Odessa our first priority was to find a place where we could live permanently. In the Soviet Union the government owned everything including housing, and people did not buy apartments; they rented—we called it "received" from the city government. Because many buildings in Odessa had been destroyed during the war, and not replaced, it was impossible to find even one room.

My parents met a man who, with his family, occupied one large room in a communal apartment, and they were going to move from Odessa. The man's daughter was a college student. My parents paid him some money as a deposit on the room, and we agreed that his daughter would share the room with us for free while she was still studying. He also had to support her by giving her some money for two or three years until her graduation; after her graduation she was supposed to leave Odessa, and we would continue to live in the room. It wasn't a good deal, but my parents didn't have a better choice.

When my brother, Roma, was transferred to the Odessa Electro-technical Institute of Communication, he joined us. Although I was seven years younger than Roma, he gave me attention, and I felt his closeness to me. I took part in some of Roma's learning and social activities. He liked music and took me to concerts of symphony music. It is to him I owe my love of classical music. Our closeness with Roma was the only positive side of living in such conditions.

The government was never able to solve the housing problem in the Soviet Union. A continued sharp shortage of housing was a part of the Soviet reality, especially in postwar time, and frequently two or more families were forced to share an apartment meant for only one family; sometimes a family of three or four persons occupied each room. Soviet people called such apartments "communal apartments." So our family plus the man's daughter were going to occupy the room for a long while.

The house we lived in was a three-story building that belonged to a paper manufacturer in pre-Soviet times. When the business was thriving, the first floor apparently served for business purposes, the second floor was for the manufacturer's family, and the third floor, at least partially, was for maids and servants. Our room was located on the second floor in the yard wing. It was not an ordinary room. It was large: six meters by eight meters (forty-eight square meters or nearly 500 square feet) and had an oval shape. One "corner" of the room had a big three-fold Venetian window with a glass door to the round balcony.

The window faced the small yard, which was surrounded by four three-story walls and looked like a well. For this reason even in the daytime, the room was rather dark. In the other "corner" of the room was the stove which was tiled with high-quality decorative tiles. The ceiling had colored stucco molding along the room perimeter with paintings on the central part. An old brass chandelier hung in the middle of the ceiling. The floor had nice varicolored wooden parquet.

Apparently, in the past, the room served as an evening parlor or as a hall in which to dance. But we weren't going to dance. We had to live in this beautiful room or to be more accurate, to live in the one-room palace without any facilities.

In the fall of 1948, I became a student of the sixth grade at the school for boys. I had no problems with any of my subjects, with the exception of, perhaps, Ukrainian. Like most schools in the city, the school was a Russian language school, and teachers taught all disciplines in Russian.

Living in Siberia, I didn't study the Ukrainian language, as those in Ukraine were required to do, therefore the school administration excused me from Ukrainian classes for three years, meaning that those years I would spend learning the language. For three years I did not even think about it. My troubles with the language didn't start until the ninth grade, as it was then that I had no choice but to take Ukrainian classes, and had to write essays, to be examined in the language, without anyone indulging me. I realized that something urgent had to be done.

I don't know why, but one of my cousins was reputed the best expert in Ukrainian in our family, and after my mother's request he became my "emergency teacher." Every day for two or three months he gave me dictations, and, as a result, I managed to pass all the tests and examinations with good marks in both Ukrainian language and Ukrainian literature. However, now I can't speak the language—I have lost what little Ukrainian I ever knew.

I don't remember most of my middle school teachers, but one of them I do remember. She was an enthusiastic teacher and liked her work. She organized a school puppet theater, and I became one of the puppet actors. The wonderful thing about her puppet theater was that the students did everything.

We (with the help of adults) constructed a special wooden stage to which we attached a simple mechanism that opened two sides of the curtain like wings. Some students modeled clay masks and then made puppets' heads from glued paper; others, using special techniques, made puppet faces, and then we tailored puppet dresses and bodies and played roles. Teachers, mainly our instructor, along with students modified many favorite tales in plays for puppet shows.

We played in many city schools and sometimes went on tour outside the city and participated in competitions. Our "troupe" even managed to make a little money and we were able to cover some necessary expenses. The show was a great success. Children liked all our performances and looked forward to new ones. One competition award (a book with written recognition) I kept for many years. When we left the USSR I saved only the page with the award inscription.

I remember most of my teachers as role models, but one middle school teacher stuck in my memory as an opposite illustration. He was a teacher who came from one of the Soviet Central Asian republics. I am not sure if he really was a teacher or just a "bird of passage." This "educator" knew neither history nor the Russian language. Unfortunately, it would be impossible to translate exactly his funny "pearls" that he pompously spoke in broken Russian.

Here is just one of these "pearls." Describing the actions of one of the ancient Russian czars, he quoted the czar's words as: "You, yourself, are kinging, continue to king, but don't put your nose in our business, otherwise as we will press you quick, and you are dead." That's supposed to mean something like this: "You are ruling, continue doing so, but don't get involved in our state affairs. Otherwise our response will be prompt and severe." We had a lot of fun mimicking him even in our responses during the tests.

Fortunately, very soon, when we were close to graduation, the school administration fired the "pearl speaker" and introduced us to another historian. He was blind, a war veteran. I don't know if he graduated from college before or after the war, but his lessons were truly artful. To tell the truth, we were not an ideal class—postwar children, we were a class of hooligans. No one cared about anybody or anything, but during his classes the silence was so deep that we could hear our neighbor's breath.

At the time when I graduated from seventh grade, we had three seventh-grade classes. After graduation, many students applied to technical schools, called "Tekhnicum," to become technicians. The remaining students were combined into one class and continued learning. I still remember most of the teachers who taught me in senior classes. Almost all of them had something that was associated with their personalities. I see them alive before my eyes.

One of them a person with a choleric temperament—he was quick like mercury. His legs and arms were in constant motion. Explaining a geometrical theorem he jumped from one corner of the classroom to another saying, "This is one diagonal; this is the second diagonal," and he continued his pirouettes with the grace of a dancer.

Another teacher, when getting angry threw a bundle of keys on his desk. The bundle usually bounced from his desk and flew under somebody's bench. We were delightfully glad to get the bundle and to bring it to him; then the procedure, as ritual, was repeated time and again.

The chemistry teacher was a knowledgeable and demanding person. He was the only teacher who forced us to keep detailed notes for each of his lectures. Later on, we realized that he taught us a university-level course of chemistry, and it served me well because by the time I left to go to the institute (university)—after I graduated from the school—I knew chemistry well. However, at that time we thought we knew better what we needed and were not so happy with his demands. We used every opportunity to do nasty things to him like putting nails in his pockets or gumming the pages of his books. He also had a habit of taking off his galoshes when coming to the classroom, and once, at break time, we managed to nail his galoshes down. It was a miracle that he did not get injured when he fell.

We had a couple of teachers with interesting personalities. One of them was an educated, no-nonsense person. His speech was a real performance—colorful, with many metaphors and epithets. We liked to make jokes mimicking him. I remember one such episode. It was during our class hours, when one of our classmates speaking with the student next to him, laughed loudly. The teacher asked him in his usual manner, "Why are you neighing, my mettlesome steed?" The brave guy immediately answered mimicking the teacher's style and intonation, "A donkey cheerfully asked." All the class burst into laughter. The teacher became speechless, and then, without uttering a word, pointed him to the door.

I liked most of my classmates and teachers and was taking my classes willingly. Because of this I had no particular reasons to skip classes, and so my parents had no need to check on me with my teachers or my class advisor. Besides, they worked long hours and had busy lives. My mother, not to mention father, had hardly ever visited my school.

One morning—the first and only time in my life I was ever late for school—I met my classmate. He wasn't a good student, and he disliked having to attend school, preferring to do fun things, like going to movies. He asked if I would like to join him at the movies and I readily agreed.

What I didn't know was that on that day, coincidentally, my mother decided to visit the school for the first time in many years. Thus, she discovered my absence. Being at the movies I was unaware of this. That night, after supper she asked me casually if there was anything interesting in school that day. I lied inspirationally… She didn't punish me, but my embarrassment and shame were worse than any punishment. I got a lesson for a lifetime.

Nine

Gambling

1956

I was admitted to Odessa Polytechnic Institute in 1954. The first college years are usually hard for most students, and I wasn't an exception. Those years were extremely busy and intense. I felt pretty tired and when the summer vacation began, I decided to take a trip. Never having traveled before, I chose to go to Kiev, the capital of Ukraine. Some of my relatives lived in Kiev, and I was going to stay with them. Kiev is a river port city, so I had an opportunity to reach Kiev by water, namely the river Dnepr. My plan was to take a small sea ship from Odessa to the city of Kherson, then a steamboat from Kherson to Kiev. The old, little exotic river ship, the scenic Dnepr coasts, and the summer weather promised a wonderful and interesting four-day trip.

The first part of the cruise was quiet and enjoyable. I loved the sea and a lot of sun. I shared a cabin with a friendly smiling man, who was much older than I. One day, after I had made an inspection of the ship and was sitting on the upper deck, I saw my cabin-mate. He came over to me, made a little small talk, and then suggested we play a game of cards. He could feel I was unenthusiastic, so he hurriedly added that we would play only for fun, for a fraction of a kopeck (a penny). I did not like to gamble, especially for money, and I had rarely played cards, but reluctantly agreed to his offer, not wanting to seem impolite.

Two men I had never met before watched us playing, and they eventually asked if they could join the game. Without bothering to break money into change, they sat down and offered to keep the score. One of them had placed on the table a piece of paper and a shiny cigarette case with an opened polished lid. I would not say that I had my heart in the game; nevertheless, I missed the point when the stakes began to rise.

I don't remember for how long we played, but I soon began to feel bored and hungry, so I decided to get out. I asked what the balance was, how much I had won, or how much I owed. The strangers did some calculations then they named an amount. My first thought was that I had misheard: the amount they stated was almost all the money I had for my vacation. I didn't mishear. I said that I didn't have such money in my pocket right now. My cabin-mate smiled and said, "It is okay, I will pay your debt. You can repay me later when we meet in the cabin." Understandably, my mood was completely spoiled. I did not want to go anywhere. I lost my appetite.

During the game I noticed a man watching us. He wasn't very young, and he looked like a former athlete, or a military officer. When the first two men who played with me told me what I owed, he stood, approached us and asked if he could join the game. My cabin-mate made an agreeable gesture. The man sat down and took a cigarette from the cigarette case, turning it a little. He told the others that low stakes were for suckers, so they raised them many times.

His movements were quick and the game began to spin with high speed. After a while, he stood up saying that he wanted to quit the game. His winnings were big, and the two men began to protest, declaring that they had lost all their money, and that they wanted to play until they had won it back. The man looked at me and told them that he would forgive them their debt if they forgave mine. Their loss was higher than mine, and realizing that they really had no choice, they agreed to the offer. Then, the man nodded to me: "Let us go get a bite to eat."

In the buffet, he told me that the guys were card sharks, and that they had been cheating me. There were decorating mirrors behind me, and they intentionally placed the cigarette case in such a way that the cigarette case's lid reflected almost all my cards… They taught me a lesson. Later on, when I traveled a lot on business trips, some of my co-travelers asked me many times to join a card game just to kill time. Remembering the lesson, I never ever did it again. Besides, I didn't see much fun in gambling—it bored me.

The "pleasant" meeting with the card sharks wasn't my last adventure in my trip to Kiev. I remember another episode from this trip, when someone tried to rob me. It happened near Khreschatik Street, the main street in Kiev. It was not too late, just early evening, when I was going home to where I was staying. I turned from Khreschatik Street to a cross street, whose name I don't recall, and came across an ordinary-looking man, much taller than I. He came close to me, showed me a large knife and said in a low voice, "Watch and money." It was so unexpected that I had no time to be really scared. Besides, I had nothing to lose: The poor college student had no money and no watch, and I told him so. He looked at me with suspicion, but I wore a T-shirt, and it was visible that I had no watch. Apparently to make sure, he felt my pockets, then, without another word, he hid the knife and left. At that time, there was no one else on the street. To be fair, I should say that most big cities were relatively safe, and incidents like these were rare. That meeting was just my personal "good" luck.

Ten

My Father

1957

In 1956, my brother, Roma, became a student of the Leningrad (now St. Petersburg) postgraduate school and moved there, one of Russia's most beautiful cities. I had been planning a trip to Moscow and Leningrad for the next year and hoped that with Roma being there I wouldn't have much trouble finding accommodations in Leningrad. But my plans did not come to realization. A terrible event shook our family and caused a lot of pain and many difficulties for years to come.

It was June 1957. I was sitting at my desk, preparing for the next examination in the college (institute). My mother was ill: she had received a vaccination for smallpox, and her body reacted with a high temperature. The fever was so severe that she would periodically lose consciousness and become delirious.

My father was sick too. He had thrombophlebitis in his leg and he lay in another bed in the same room. Between their beds, there was a folding wooden screen, and it was closed over, so they couldn't see each other. I don't know exactly what happened with Mother when she suddenly screamed loudly. I think she may just have been delirious. In fear for her, Father jumped out from the bed but couldn't stand up and collapsed backwards. I rushed to Dad, hugged him and asked what happened. I saw that something was terribly wrong, but there was nothing I could do. As doctors diagnosed it later, the jump appeared to be fatal: the thrombus in his leg was torn away and clogged the artery to his lung.

At first when Father collapsed, I looked at him not fully understanding what was going on. I thought that he had simply lost consciousness and immediately called the ambulance. A doctor arrived quickly. After a short examination he told me that Father had died. I couldn't believe it. I shook the doctor's shoulders, repeatedly shouting that this couldn't be true. Father died in my arms, looking in my eyes. My whole life I will remember how his blue eyes were glazing over, while he tried to tell me something. I loved my father very much and never could imagine that something, especially something like that, could happen to him.

The doctor wrote down a medical conclusion and went away. He told me privately that to avoid the autopsy and other complications, he would state that the cause of death was a heart attack, and not lung thrombosis. What difference did it make? I couldn't think clearly and was acting automatically. I managed to call some relatives, and when they came, somebody covered all the mirrors in the room with sheets; it is a kind of tradition to cover the mirrors in a house when somebody dies.

Father's death was a huge loss for our family, for all of us; he was irreplaceable. We lost a man for whom his family was first priority, his main concern and care. He had survived extremely hard times: the times of the October overturn and havoc in 1917, the time of the starvation, and the years of war and repression. To support our family he worked day and night, though he never complained. Father and Mother married in 1927, and they remained together for thirty years, until his untimely death. Father always was a loving and devoted husband. Mother survived Father by over twenty-five years, and she never got over his death. He was also a loving and devoted father for us, his children, and although he didn't have a chance of gaining a higher education, he was a clever man and generously shared with us his life experience. He was our friend and advisor, and all of our numerous relatives and friends loved him for his kindness, his wit, and his constant willingness to help.

I couldn't sleep at all that night. When Mother opened her eyes the next day and saw the covered mirrors, she instantly understood what had happened. She began to cry so hysterically that we wanted to call the ambulance again. It took a long time to calm her down.

I was in a haze all that day. People were coming and going constantly, and eventually I felt exhausted. I sat on a bed and all of a sudden fell soundly asleep. My cousin told me later that I slept for almost twenty-four hours, and then they started to worry. They woke me once and then, opening my eyes for a moment I fell asleep again. Finally, they woke me again about ten or twelve hours later. I have little memory of how I managed to continue my examinations, or how I completed the session.

My father
Relatives, friends, coworkers loved him

Eleven

The Compromise

1958

During my years at the college (institute), and even after graduation, I constantly looked for an opportunity to earn some extra money, which was needed to support my family. In Odessa, it was always difficult to find an additional part-time job. In most cases the only available work was as a loader at the city's seaport or tutoring students. I knew that one thing I could do well—it was tutoring which I did any time I could get a job. Gradually I earned a good reputation, and people started to refer me to college students who needed some extra help.

Tutoring was generally a routine work for me, but a couple of cases were associated with something unusual. One of such case about a young man, a student (I don't remember his name) I would like to mention. He was in his final year at one of the Odessa institutes and had some difficulties with his diploma project. According to his words, his parents were relatively prosperous people, and they were willing to pay good money to anybody who could help him. Actually, what my visitor wanted was for somebody to do the project for him, from the beginning to the end, and, indeed, he mentioned a considerable amount of money as a payment, even offering to pay more than half of it in advance. Payment wasn't an issue for him.

I looked over the details of the diploma assignment and requirements and spoke with the young man. I realized that the project concerned the HV (heating and ventilation) field, and that wasn't difficult. So, the project itself wasn't a problem. The problem was that my visitor had many serious gaps in his knowledge of main subjects.

It was the first time I had received such an unusual offer for my service. I used to help in small jobs, like course work and projects, but that was a big piece of work: the whole diploma project. I felt uncomfortable; there was something I didn't like: it wasn't real tutoring. First of all, it was inappropriate and therefore undesirable. Secondly, I could do the whole project from A to Z by myself, but he simply wouldn't be able to understand his own project, which he, and only he, was to present and answer all questions on. I thought, "How is he going to do that?" By solving one problem, he was creating a new one which was in some sense even harder than the first. Although the offer was tempting it wasn't acceptable for me.

I thought for a while before finally making up my mind, and I told my "customer" that I would accept the work, but under some essential conditions. I would teach him all the theoretical and practical matters related to the project, and I was prepared to explain them as many times as was necessary for him to understand. Also, I would explain to him each formula and the numbers which he should use in the project calculations, and that I would check everything—his understanding, his calculations, his drawings—and make necessary corrections. My main condition was: the job had to be done by his but nobody else's hands—it was the only compromise I could accept. I was aware that there was little time left for the project, so I was ready to meet him three or four times a week. The guy agreed, although I didn't see great enthusiasm on his face.

Only when the work had begun I completely realized the burden I had placed on my shoulders. I knew that it wouldn't be easy, but his gaps in all subjects were considerably bigger than I expected. Sometimes I wondered how he managed to finish eight semesters with such huge gaps. I spent a great deal of time repeating many things, checking and correcting each step over and over again. Nevertheless, I wasn't sorry and didn't retreat. At least, I did my best, and, finally, three months later, the project was completed. My student showed the project to his official supervisor, received an approval, and I took a long breath.

I was surprised when, two weeks after his graduation, the young man came to my home. He brought a huge bouquet of flowers, a cake, and an envelope with additional money. He was so happy that he was shining like the summer sun. He thanked me many times, and he told me that his diploma work had become, unexpectedly, his best institute experience. To his astonishment, while defending the project, he answered almost all the questions and graduated successfully. It seemed to me I felt no less happy and proud than my student. My decision was really a decision worthy of Solomon.

Twelve

My First Engineering Project

1959

When I began my work for the heat/gas department of "Ukrstroyproekt," which is the Russian acronym of the Ukrainian Engineering Design Company, I was the youngest person in the department. Most of the employees were women in their thirties and forties. They called me by a diminutive nickname (Semochka) and treated me like their child or a younger brother. Gradually, as time passed, my relationships with my coworkers developed into friendships. I worked with the company for five years, and due to my warm and friendly relationship with my managers and many of my coworkers, I recall that time with pleasure.

My first design project was an ordinary engineering work. I had to design a small boiler house with low-capacity boilers. To my surprise, my first steps in design work were not as easy as I had expected. For one whole working day, I sat in front of a sheet of Whatman (drawing paper) and didn't have a clue from what to start. I found that I had a vague idea about design requirements, rules, and regulations. However, pretty soon I learned how to do these things and no longer found them difficult and complex.

After a while, despite my involvement in various projects my work became less exciting and more familiar and routine, sometimes even boring. I lost some of my initial interest in it. I was looking for something new and challenging. When the chief of my department called a meeting to announce that we had been offered a new and unusual project, something fundamentally different from what we usually designed before, I was eager to learn more details about the job. I learned that the project was connected with power plant reconstruction and retrofitting. The job wasn't routine and sounded attractive to me. So, when the chief offered me the project engineer assignment, I was happy and looked forward to starting.

This was to become my first real engineering project, on which I was responsible for both the basic engineering solutions and the important administrative decisions related to the project. Of course, I believed that nobody would refuse to give me advice, if I asked for it, but my managers expected that I would do the job on my own. Naturally, I was full of new feelings and emotions. For a better understanding of my excitement, I think it is necessary to provide a few more details and explain briefly the issue of the project.

The project centered on an old, low-capacity power plant in the city of Ismail, a small river port city. In the recent past, the city had been the capital of the Ismail region (oblast). Later on the city and all the former regional territories were included into the Odessa region, and Ismail lost its capital status. Odessa authorities wanted to close the power plant because of its poor performance and outdated, ineffective equipment. Despite all of this, the Regional Energy Agency and Ismail authorities were interested in keeping the power plant operating. The employment of many people and the Regional Energy Agency's existence depended on that power plant. So, the problem we encountered was how to save the inefficient and obsolete power plant at minimum cost. The power plant was so old and out-of-date that even the plant's building couldn't be used. The only way to save that plant was to increase its effectiveness without spending a considerable amount of money on reconstruction. It was a creative and challenging problem.

I went on a business trip to Ismail being full of thoughts and worries: it was my first independent business trip, and I had to meet high-ranking people and discuss serious matters with them. Indeed, after my first meeting with the mayor of Ismail and the chief engineer of the power plant I felt exhausted. The city and power plant administrations expected me to come up with a ready-to-work solution. Alas, I did not even have feasible ideas worthy of discussion. While preparing for the business trip, I spent several days in libraries doing research and also discussed the matter with knowledgeable engineers, but no solutions or suggestions offered were practical.

The solution came unexpectedly, after I had returned to Odessa. As I pondered on how to increase the efficiency of the power plant, I realized that it could be achieved by combining the generation of electricity with the utilization of low-temperature heat. That simple solution allowed me to kill two birds with one stone. Total efficiency of the power system (power plant plus greenhouse heaters) could be considerably increased. Additionally, the city would receive the benefit of environmental improvement and a solution to the problem of future residential heating and hot water supply.

Although it wasn't a big innovation, undoubtedly, it was a good, economical solution. The "Power Plant" project was successful, and I received a commendation and a small barrel of wine from the power plant officials. While giving me the wine, the chief engineer told me that a special winery, which was located in the Ismail region, supplied the Kremlin with that high-quality wine. The plant had just received several barrels of that wine from the farm director as a special present. I have to admit that the wine was really good. My friends, whom I treated with that divine drink, liked it very much and regretted it when we finished the barrel.

The years of my work with "Ukrstroyproekt" coincided with the beginning of the total transition of Odessa and Odessa region enterprises from coal and oil burning to natural gas. It was a relatively new area and many accompanying problems were emerging all the time. Working for my company, I constantly looked for challenging and creative projects. I liked it much more than routine design work. My boss and my supervisor knew about my desire to do something challenging, and they sympathized with my wishes.

Later on, I was involved in many other challenging and, perhaps much more interesting projects, but I still remember the "Power Plant" project because it was the first one and, maybe, because of…Kremlin wine.

Thirteen

The Fight

1960

I always preferred to spend vacations with my friends, but when I began to work, most of my friends had already graduated from their institutes and universities and left the city. Besides, I had a limited choice of where to go for a vacation. My company received several tourist packages to a Caucasian mountain lake, called Gyok-Gyol, which was located in the Caucasian republic of Azerbaijan, near the Armenian border.

I bought the travel package and joined the tour. As it was scheduled, I spent about a week in the camp near the lake. It was a nice, spectacular tourist place with beautiful views of preserved pieces of wilderness.

I enjoyed the tour, but not everything was always so pleasant. I witnessed an example of the ethnic hatred prevalent in the area, something I hadn't expected to see. Soviet propaganda always proclaimed brotherhood and friendship across the different ethnic groups and nationalities, and on the surface it looked to be the truth. However, as I was to find out later, all conflicts, of which there were many in the multiracial Soviet society, were kept secret and hidden under the Soviet propaganda.

Soviet authorities forced all republics, autonomies, and minority administrative units to have Russian people at the highest levels of power, and suppressed any independence of minority groups. A lot of harm had been caused by this "preferential" policy when controversies between nationalities were resolved at the expense of others. This policy provoked a veiled hatred towards Russians as well as between other nationalities. I understood it later, but then it was the first time I had ever seen racial hatred between Azerbaijani and Armenians.

An Armenian football team was resting at our camp. They had their own tent where they lived. They were friendly guys, and frequently my tent-mates and I would spend half of the night talking and joking with them.

The camp had a dance stage where young men and women danced every evening. Local Azerbaijani guys frequently came to the dances, and their behavior was rude and abusive. I don't remember exactly how their fight started, but I heard two men arguing with each other. One of them was a football player, and the second one was a local guy. He was saying something offensive in their local dialect, like, "We don't need you f... dirty Armenians over here; we will show you your place." I didn't pay much attention to the quarrel because I didn't believe that it could be anything serious, especially since the local man left.

That evening, after the dancing, one of the players invited me to the football players' tent to chat a little. In the middle of our conversation, I suddenly heard loud voices outside the tent and saw strained expression on the faces of the fellows with whom I spoke. I couldn't understand what was going on because it wasn't Russian speech. In a moment, my tent-mates put me in the center of the tent, and before I could ask what was happening, I heard heavy blows on the tent and somebody was groaning. People began hurriedly running out. It was dark outside. I tried to get out of the tent as well, but two players restrained me, protecting me and not allowing me to move. They warned me not to get out of the tent: I could be badly hurt.

I heard furious fighting outside the tent. Somebody called the militia (the Soviet police). When they arrived and I was allowed to get out, I saw several badly wounded players. It appeared that the local men came with thick long steel rods and began striking people with the rods. Because of the tent, we couldn't see what was going on and were helpless to defend ourselves. Miraculously nobody got killed although a couple of players were seriously injured.

At that time I hadn't yet realized how deep the national, or maybe religious, hatred was between the people of the two republics. Later on, during a business trip in Armenia, I discussed the incident with my Armenian colleague. He explained to me something about the Nagorno-Karabakh region where the population was almost a hundred percent Armenian. The Soviet government made the whole region a part of the Azerbaijanian Republic against the will of the Armenian people. It created a problem, which, later on, during the Gorbachev era ended with the Armenian massacre in the Nagorno-Karabakh region and the city of Baku.

Fourteen

Hotel Adventures

1960 to 1964

I worked for a design company, gradually gaining experience in not only the area of design but in many other aspects of professional life. One such valuable experience was from business trips during which I got to know many useful things. Most of my business trips were more or less educational and, sometimes, stressful. Now, some of those "stressful" trips I can't recall without a smile.

A difficult part of practically all my business and non-business trips was finding a place to stay. Due to an extreme shortage of hotels in Soviet cities and towns, we, ordinary engineers and many times not ordinary ones as well, didn't have the luxury of hotel reservations. On many occasions, the first day of a trip had to be spent in search of a place to stay.

I remember my first business trip to Moscow. I had heard that Moscow, the capital of the country and a large city, had, compared to other Soviet cities, an unusually high number of hotels, so I was absolutely sure that I didn't have to worry where I would sleep at night. I arrived in the city in the early morning and began to work my way through a list of where I was told I had the best chance to check in. The response everywhere was standard: "Sorry, we have no vacancies, at least, until the end of the week." Actually, I didn't often hear the word "sorry"—just dry "no vacancies." I decided not to waste any more time. I wanted to do some business and then try again later, after work. The evening was as "successful" as the morning. My last attempt was late in the evening and I was tired. Then, I recalled the advice someone gave me about trying the Moscow State University student campus. For as young as I was at that time, it could have worked. It was my last option and last hope. I rushed to the campus.

The university campus appeared to be huge, filled with many buildings both large and small, their managers and administrators with whom I could speak had already gone home, and I didn't know what to do. I found a group of five-story buildings, which seemed to have more activity than the others. They were student dormitories, and one of them had a bench near the entry. I sat down on the bench, put my suitcase next to me and thought, "Well, if nothing better, I will spend the night on the bench."

Apparently, I was getting drowsy when I heard steps, and then saw a girl approaching me. "Are you okay? What's the matter with you?" she asked. I told her what the matter was with me, with the hotel service, with our life, and with the whole world. The girl was laughing. "I like your dark humor. Let me see what I can do to help you," she said and went into the dormitory. Usually dormitories had separate floors for male and female students, and I thought she would ask for help from the male students. Nobody was going into or coming out of the building. I had waited ten or fifteen minutes before the girl appeared again. She brought a male student ID and gave it to me. Then, she took my suitcase and said, "Follow me. Don't get close to the security guard. Just show him the ID and hurry to get out of his sight." I did exactly that.

When we got to her room the light was off, and I could barely see the silhouettes in the darkness. It was a room for seven or eight students, and all the girls were already sleeping in their beds. Silently, my angel-rescuer showed me to the vacant bed where I could sleep, and she herself shared a bed with her roommate. Tired, I immediately fell asleep.

The problems began the next morning. I woke because I needed to use the bathroom, and as I opened my eyes, I could see that some of the girls were awake and sitting around the room, and some others were still sleeping. I closed my eyes again, not knowing what to do, but after a while I knew I couldn't wait any longer and, keeping my eyes closed, I begged in a whisper that I needed to get out. They heard me, and as the girls laughed they turned away from me and told me I was free to get up.

The next two days my searches for hotels were totally fruitless, and two more nights I used the hospitality of my kind girls. By the end of the third day I even knew some of their names. My farewell with the girls was warm and full of laughter.

That wasn't my only adventure concerning hotels. A couple of years later, I had a business trip to the Saratov Gas Research Institute. It was the wintertime and, as always, I worried about hotels. The city of Saratov was the center of the Saratov oblast (region); nevertheless, it still was a provincial city with three or four small hotels to serve the whole city. The chief of my department told me that the Gas Research Institute had its own small shelter with two or three rooms for business travelers, but they only made reservations for some special occasions. Since I couldn't make a reservation I could only hope for the best.

At that time the air transportation between Odessa and Saratov was unreliable and inconvenient, especially in the winter. In addition, most journeys necessitated at least one or two plane changes. Sometimes, depending on weather conditions, a journey by air could take even longer than going by the train. The trip to Saratov took two nights, and I arrived in the city in the morning. My attempts to get a hotel were, of course, unsuccessful, and I hurried up to the Gas Institute. After meeting with the engineer I wanted to meet with, I asked for help with their shelters. They didn't have any vacant places in their only shelter, and that included even the corridor. The situation appeared to be worse than I expected. I felt I had no option but to go to the railway station.

On my way to the railway station I pondered over my chances of finding any accommodation for the night and came to the unfortunate conclusion that the situation was hopeless, so I decided to head for home even though I had unfinished business in the city.

The terminal was overcrowded. There was an unbearable stench of sweat, smoke and food in the air. It seemed that there wasn't any oxygen at all. In addition, it was impossible to find a vacant place to sit even for a few minutes. Many people were lying on the dirty terminal floor, stretching newspapers or coats under themselves.

The only option of getting back home was a single train that passed through the station, and it was necessary to buy a ticket for that train. According to the schedule, I had a couple of hours to wait before the train pulled in so I joined the long line of people waiting for tickets. Over the period of a half hour maybe only a dozen tickets were sold, no more. Some people were lucky, but I wasn't one of them. So, one way or another, I managed to wait until the morning and left from there for the city airport.

To my disappointment, when I arrived there I realized that the airplanes hadn't flown in two days because of the severe weather conditions, and the forecast for the next couple of days didn't leave me with much hope. I returned to the city and repeated my hotel search tour all over again. "Success" in all hotels was the same. Again, I went to the railway station, hoping that this time I would be closer to the cashier's window. Not a chance: a lot of people were already in a long line waiting for tickets, and the train was late by several hours. I was desperate for any ticket, for any chance of getting back home. Unfortunately, bad luck was chasing me—all available tickets were sold long before I reached the cashier. Hoping to take a free ride, I rushed to the platform. The train was supposed to have a fifteen- to twenty-minute stop. When I got to the platform, I saw how even people with tickets had to rush to the train cars to have a chance of getting on.

The sun had already begun to rise, and I returned to the terminal and found a vacant place on a terminal bench, where I tried in vain to take a nap. My head was empty: no thoughts, no wishes—I felt sick. Two cups of hot coffee helped just for a while, then I felt dizzy again. My head was in a haze; I lost my sense of time and suddenly it was dusk. I didn't notice how dusk came. I was thinking about my uncompleted business, about my work and coworkers. All of a sudden I recalled that when I was leaving my office, my coworker gave me the telephone number of one of his old wartime friends who happened to live in Saratov. During the war they fought together, and he asked me to call him just to say "Hello."

I dialed the number, and luckily, the man was home. I conveyed my coworker's wishes to him, and he asked me where I was calling from and why my voice was so low. I told him that I was calling from the terminal, that I hadn't slept for two nights, and a third sleepless night would kill me. He realized immediately what was going on and told me to stay where I was. Shortly afterwards, he arrived at the terminal in a taxi and took me to his home.

When we arrived at his home, his wife prepared a good supper, serving it with half a glass of vodka. I don't remember whether I had enough energy to finish the food. I fell on the bed and in a split second was dead to the world. I slept for over twenty-four hours and woke up feeling reborn. The next day I completed what business I had left to finish, and my rescuer and now my new friend helped me buy a ticket to Odessa. I was never so happy to be going home.

I have to say that during my working career I had more than a few stressful business trips. When these stressful situations were related to business I took them as a necessary part of the business, and they didn't stick in my memory for as long as those small funny incidents. Nevertheless, the small things are also part, and frequently the biggest part, of our life and they are worth mentioning.

Fifteen

Marriage

1960 to 1963

After graduation from the college I kept in touch with Sasha Fishman, a former student of the same college with whom I had a friendly relationship during our college years. He worked for the company "Institut Avtomatiki." Sometimes he called me; sometimes I used to drop by his place, but I had never attended any entertainment events with him and his wife before. Nevertheless, when they unexpectedly invited me to see a new play in our local drama theater, I accepted the invitation with pleasure.

It was a première of a play, called *104 Pages About Love*. Sasha told me that they had only one extra ticket. Initially I paid no heed to his words, and only afterwards I realized that he told me that to ensure that I would come alone. Coming to the theater, I found Sasha with his wife, Nelya, and a girl approximately my age sitting in the box, and the girl's seat happened to be next to mine. Sasha introduced me to the girl, saying that she was his coworker. The girl's name was Susanna.

The play was great, but the rest was even greater: when the curtain finally fell, Sasha told me that he hoped I wouldn't let Susanna go home alone. Again, he didn't leave me a choice, but in any case, I was going to do so. It was not late, and the night was warm and pleasant; Susanna's home was within walking distance from the theater; thus, we decided to walk. I don't remember the specifics of what we talked about—it was just general chitchat.

This "accidental" meeting had no continuation. After that meeting in the theater, we (really accidentally) met once again when my business took me to the company where Susanna worked. After that, we did not see each other for almost two years. I was busy with many things: new projects on my work and Mother's illness, which became chronic and required a lot of my attention and support. I continued my self-education and whenever I got the chance I did a little extra work for some additional money. Sometimes I managed to date girls, though I didn't have much time for a personal life.

One weekend, while I was preparing for the next business trip, I went downtown to find a shop to repair my raincoat. While there and unexpectedly, I met Susanna on the corner of Ekaterininskaya Street and Deribasovskaya Street. Almost two years had passed since our first meeting in the theater where we became acquainted. We immediately recognized each other and chatted for over an hour.

What sticks in my memory is that a famous satirical actor, Arkady Raykin, was touring the city and appearing on the local TV station at the time. Susanna mentioned that she would like to watch the show, but neither she nor I had a TV set, although I did have friends where we could go to watch it. It was the beginning of the Soviet TV era, and only a few people had a TV set (and, of course, only black and white). I am not sure whether we really asked anybody about Raykin's show, but we arranged a day to meet again. So we started dating, and as far as I remember, we dated no more than three or four times between my business trips.

One of my business trips was to west Ukraine to the city of Lvov. It was not a long trip, only four or five days, but they were busy days filled with work and endless meetings, and I was barely able to free a couple of hours each evening to see the sights or do anything else. Walking down one street, I saw a shop that sold funny ceramic toys. I bought one for Susanna. I missed her. I had dated girls before, but it was something different this time, more serious and deeper. As one would say: the chemistry was different. I am cautious in my choice of words because to love a woman is a special feeling, and here the word "love" is a special word. In short—"love is a love" is the best definition.

When I returned and met up with Susanna I asked her to marry me, and she accepted. She also expressed her wish that I come to her home and ask her parents' permission, maybe their blessing, to take their daughter's hand in marriage. I read about such things in old classic literature, and Susanna's unexpected wish sounded a little unusual, funny, and at the same time quite touching. In any event, a wish was a wish. I agreed without any comments.

My visit to her family was a great experience. I put on my best and only suit with a modest tie so that my attire suited the event and went to Susanna's place. When I dated Susanna she was twenty-six, had worked for over four years, and was financially secure and independent, but like almost all young people in this country, she didn't have her own place to live and shared an apartment with her parents. I am saying "apartment" because actually it was two rooms in an eight-room apartment with a tiny kitchen, bathroom and toilet which were common for all residents. During the Soviet era, it was frequent for several unrelated families to share an apartment.

Four families, numbering over ten people occupied Susanna's apartment. (Later, when I lived there, the number of occupants increased to fourteen). Each facility had four electrical switches, and the number of switches was equal to the number of occupying families. Again, those were not unusual living conditions. When I arrived at Susanna's place, the first thing I saw was a set of four electrical door bells. I carefully selected one of the buttons and after a couple of minutes Susanna opened the door.

She introduced me to her parents. Her father, Grigory Ovseevich, was a short, bald gentleman with a kind, friendly smile. Her mother, Fanya Isaevna, a no-nonsense woman with dark brown eyes and gray hair, was smiling as well and pretending that she did not know the real reason for my visit.

The dinner was nice. We talked about different things, and I couldn't find the right moment to ask what I was supposed to ask. After a while, the silent expectancy hung in the air. I could only guess how awkward I looked. Finally I made up my mind, and after the second or third dish, I dived in and came up from the cold water: I announced that Susanna and I were to be married, and I was here to ask for her parents' blessing. Susanna's parents encouragingly smiled, which meant apparently that we were given the blessing.

As I was going to fly to Leningrad because of Mother's forthcoming surgery, we decided to register our marriage at the end of December on my return from my trip. Besides, to make my mother feel better I wanted to tell her the news before the formal registration. I knew she was looking forward to seeing me married and would be pleasantly excited with such good news.

After a short while, I flew to Leningrad in order to help Mother before and especially after the surgery. We all looked forward to the surgery with hope, expecting that it would help Mom a lot, and even though she was a little nervous she remained in a good mood. I told her about my intention to get married and the proposal that I had made. Of course, she had a lot of questions, and I told her about Susanna and Susanna's parents.

My parents were open-minded and tolerant people, and they taught us to be the same. However, when it came to speaking of her sons' future wives and what she expected of their personalities, education, age and appearance, my mother made much more of two particular things: social status and family, including close relatives (as it called in Yiddish, "Mishpukha"). As for many parents of her age, consciously or unconsciously, nationality was not of the least importance to her, though there were happy mixed marriages in our "mishpukha." Being young and having little life experience, I personally did not pay much attention to such matters as origin, communality of interests and cultures, relatives, etc. Later on life taught me many things, and I understood better what Mother meant and why it was so important for her. When Mother got to know Susanna, she loved and treated her like her daughter.

Generally, the surgery was successful. Mother felt a good bit better, though right after the operation it was too soon to tell how complete the recovery of the movement functions for her left arm and leg would be.

I had already used up all my time off, and when Mother left the hospital, I returned home. We believed it would be better if Mother stayed in Leningrad till her full recovery and then come back to Odessa sometime between January and February of 1963, as soon as she was able to move. I returned to Odessa around the middle of November.

At that time, one couldn't submit an application for civil marriage and get a marriage certificate the same day. There was a mandatory thirty-day waiting period between submitting an application and receiving the actual marriage registration in case the groom and/or bride changed their minds.

Nobody in the city, with the exception of Susanna's parents, knew about our engagement; I asked my supervisor to allow me a couple of hours off. Susanna did the same, and we went to the marriage registration office. The office had a long, boring name: Bureau of the Registration of the Civil Act Statuses. This was the office where people usually submitted applications for marriages. Including the time we had to wait in line, it took two hours to submit the application. We submitted ours at the end of November, and because of the month-long waiting period our real registration was supposed to take place at the end of December. Between those two dates I had a business trip and one more event took place that we can't recall without laughing.

Mother and I shared a single but huge room in our communal apartment; the room was approximately five hundred square feet. Mother was afraid to be left alone at home while I was at work; she also needed help to get around and do things. Since my salary wasn't that good and any financial support was desirable, we used to rent part of the room to students, both boys and girls. This time, we decided that while Mom was in Odessa we would rent out the part of the room to girls.

The girls were students at different city junior colleges. The older girl was engaged and was going to get married. Her fiancé was a nice young fellow, but he happened to live in a well-known Odessa district, "Peresyp," populated by many rude and criminal people.

The young bride invited Susanna and me to her wedding. Because of poor transportation we were late in getting there. By the time we arrived, the proceedings were already in full swing, and when we entered most of the guests had already downed plenty of toasts and they were all pretty "warm." At first, the people in the room looked suspiciously at my "too intelligent" appearance for such a place, but after the newlyweds introduced us as their best friends, they began demanding that I drink all the toasts I missed. I remember that I had drunk two or three five-ounce glasses of vodka, and then I lost count. I am afraid the ability to count was not the only thing I lost that evening…

Of course, I got dead drunk. Susanna told me the next day what happened after we left the wedding. In her words, on our way home I entertained the passengers in the streetcar with all kind of drunken escapades. Susanna was forced to literally carry me home in her arms and put me to bed. I mumbled something to her about taking a short nap, and asked her to wait a while to allow me to compose myself and walk her home. In the middle of my request I fell asleep. The next day, I woke up with a terrible headache, vaguely recalling what happened the day before. Fortunately, that event did not cause any significant damage to my reputation in Susanna' eyes, though all the following years she didn't miss a chance to remind me of that "bright" episode of my biography.

We had to register our marriage at the end of December, but the last week of the year Susanna became ill. We were young and even illness could not prevent our marriage. On December 29, 1962, informing nobody about our intentions, we again took several hours off from our work, went to the Bureau of the Registration of the Civil Act Statuses and received our marriage certificate. Now the name of the office sounded much less boring. We didn't want a typical wedding reception for hundreds of guests, the type that includes not only family and friends, but almost everyone the couple happened to know and with whom they were sometimes barely acquainted. We invited a limited number of people—only our close friends—deciding to postpone the celebration of the event with relatives until my mother's full recovery and return home. Of course, Mrs. and Mr. Fishman, who introduced us to each other over two years before, were among our guests, and they felt proud of their successful matchmaking achievement.

A couple of months later when Mom got better and came back from Leningrad, we celebrated our marriage with relatives. My family life had begun.

Susanna and Solomon
Just married

Sixteen

Mother's Surgeries

1962 to 1965

After Father's death Mother got ill. With time, her health continued to deteriorate, but worst of all, she was diagnosed with Parkinson's disease. And it wasn't all. One more thing in Mother's situation depressed me badly: her symptoms of Parkinson's disease progressed fast. Doctors prescribed for her all kinds of medications, all of which had debilitating side effects, and even a small dose made her feel miserable. I did not know how to make her life easier. She needed help with walking, and each visit to a doctor was difficult and painful. Mother suffered physically and psychologically, but she did not want to give up.

I searched for new medications and treatments for her illness—even some available overseas in foreign countries—and I told her of my findings. Once I came across information in the Soviet central newspaper that doctors found how to treat the disease with surgery. When I showed Mom the newspaper with a brief notice about the first doctors in the Soviet Union who got special training in England and began to perform surgeries for Parkinson's disease, Mom was immediately taken with the idea of undergoing the operation.

Understandably, Mother's enthusiasm was just her first reaction, but the actual decision was not easy. When we met and spoke with the surgeon he explained to us that the operation would necessitate the following: a surgeon would have to incise into the brain until he reached a pinhead-sized area under the cerebellum, then he would have to kill the diseased cells present in that area.

The surgery itself was quite risky; besides, the invasive methodology of the treatment was almost experimental, technically poorly equipped, and the surgeon had limited experience. Mother was of small stature, but was a woman of strong spirit. Psychologically she was courageous and resolute.

I felt uneasy regarding the surgery, simply because of the fear that Mother could die or become totally crippled. When I tried to convince her not to undergo the operation, she cut short all discussions. She just told me that she would take her chances, that she could not and did not want to live in such misery, and that she had already made up her mind. On the other hand, I had no better options to offer.

The doctor was practicing in St. Petersburg (formerly Leningrad). None of us had any connections with the medical world, and Mother wrote a letter to my brother, Roma. He was a student at a post-graduate school in Leningrad, and once he received Mother's letter he began to look for ways to contact the surgeon. It took a lot of effort, and finally, he obtained permission for Mother's visit and then for the surgery, though the surgeon was reluctant to perform the surgery because of Mother's age: she was over fifty-five.

Mother had problems with both sides of her body, but her left arm and left leg were more afflicted with the disease than the right ones. In cases when both sides were afflicted, the operation had to be performed in two stages. From the beginning it had to be one side, and after a while, the surgery could be done on the other side of the brain. Fortunately for Mom, the risk was much less for the right side of the brain, which is responsible for the left part of the body. Taking into consideration the surgeon's lack of experience, it was psychologically easier for Mother to start with the less risky operation.

Generally, the surgery was successful. Mother felt a good bit better, though right after the operation it was too soon to tell how complete the recovery of the movement functions for her left arm and leg was.

Before her first surgery, the left side of Mother's body was performing worse than the right side, which, at that time, was more or less okay. In the back of my mind, I even hoped that one surgery would be enough. Indeed, with regard to the Parkinson's disease symptoms Mother felt much better after the first surgery. She could move her left arm and her left leg more easily, noticeably so, and her face looked more lively and spirited. But unfortunately, after a while, the right side of her body—which only three years previously looked relatively healthy—was getting worse: the right hand and right leg were becoming increasingly stiffer. She decided then to undergo the operation once more.

Consulting Mother before the first operation, her surgeon explained to us some details of the procedure. He mentioned that performing the surgery on the right hemisphere of the brain which controls the left side of the body was considerably safer than operating on the left part of the human brain which controls the right side of the body. This is due to the proximity of several vital centers located in the left cerebral hemisphere.

In those years, surgical equipment was not as sophisticated and accurate as it is nowadays, and any operation on the left side of the brain was highly risky. As I understood it, should the surgeon make even the most miniscule of inaccuracies with the equipment while close to a vital center, it could cause serious health damage, even death.

I can't recall whether the doctor made his statement regarding the risks of the operation so clear, but I was sure that Mother was aware of the possible consequences of the surgery. Understanding the risk, I was worried a lot about the surgical treatment and discussed the matter with her several times. After all discussions, she decided in favor of the "radical cure," and she did it with "open eyes." Mother was a courageous, strong-willed person. She didn't want to be a burden on us. She wanted to help us with the grandchildren and be an active member of the family and simply to have a normal life. Besides, she suffered a lot from the side effects of the medicine doctors prescribed for her to treat her symptoms. Inspired by the success of the first operation, she hoped for the best.

I arrived in Leningrad several days before the surgery, which was to take place in the same Naval Academy Hospital where Mother had had her first one. The operation lasted several hours. We were allowed to be in the recovery room a little before Mother woke up from the anesthesia. Her head and forehead were in bandages.

After a while she woke up and was trying to say something, but we couldn't understand a word: all we heard was "mooing." What we were afraid of had happened. Apparently, the "verbal" cells of Mother's brain were somehow damaged during the surgery, and the consequence was that Mother lost her ability to speak. Again and again, she tried to say something, and then suddenly, she came to realize that she couldn't speak, and she began to cry so helplessly and desperately that it was impossible to face. Why? Why her? The worst thing in the world is to see your closest and dearest people suffering and not be able to help them.

It was a difficult, sad day... I was devastated. We spoke with the surgeon. He had nothing to say; just trying to calm us down somehow, he expressed the belief that after a while she would be better.

Months later, when the brain edema dissolved, Mother's speech did improve a little bit, but still it remained hard to understand her. For that reason, she was reluctant to speak with anybody, though I was able to understand her more or less. I tried to encourage her to speak more often, hoping that exercising the verbal centers she could improve her ability to speak. But my efforts were in vain. She limited herself to a couple of essential words, even with me. I longed to be able to help her more, but regardless of how hard I tried, my attempts to do anything for her were unsuccessful: she just didn't listen to me. Unfortunately, we didn't have the luxury of a speech therapist. I left Leningrad with a heavy heart, still hoping that when she would come to live with us she would be better off.

Seventeen

Dina's Habits

1964 to 1968

The beginning of my work in the Technological Institute coincided with the birth of my daughter, Dina. When I started to work, Susanna was eight months pregnant and at the time we didn't know our child's gender. It is impossible to tell from where Susanna got this idea, but her perception was that, traditionally, the majority of fathers wanted sons and she wished hard for it. As for me, I had no preference. Anyway, there was nothing we could do. We made some preparations and waited for the delivery.

It was early in the morning when Susanna woke me up and told me that she was going to give birth. We had neither a car nor a telephone at that time. Fortunately, Susanna was able to walk, and we decided to go to the maternity hospital which was located close to our home. Dina was born the same day my father died seven years earlier. Following Jewish tradition, and in honor of my father, we gave our daughter the name Dina, which although was not similar to my father's name, David, it did at least have the same first letter.

When Dina was born I was a happy father, but I was supposed to show my happiness while staying away from the child. I was "persona non grata" at a distance closer than five feet from Dina. For the first month or so our women didn't allow me even to approach to the baby. She was so small and looked so fragile that in the beginning I was afraid to touch her, and Susanna was as afraid as I was. She and my mother-in-law took control of all the care and kept me away from the child. Nevertheless, defending my paternal rights, I managed to save a piece of oilcloth that the medical personnel had attached to Dina's hand after her birth and used as her ID in the maternity hospital. I also saved a lock of her silky blond hair. I still keep these relics in our family archive. Eleven years later, I added to my family collection Vova's hair and his oilcloth ID.

From the day of Dina's birth, she had dimples on her cheeks and looked beautiful, especially when she smiled. I could admire her all day long, but when she cried, I would get nervous: I could not stand to see her crying.

The biggest problem we encountered as new parents was feeding Dina, due mainly to a shortage of mother's milk. We didn't have a sophisticated infant food industry like that available in the United States. Instead, we had special district kitchens that prepared infant mixtures from cow's milk. There was one not far from us although it was not of a high quality nor did it provide food healthy enough for a small child, especially in the summertime. But we had no choice.

As a result of the artificial feeding, Dina got severe dyspepsia and for two weeks was under hospital treatment. Like any other family with a newborn child our days were filled with duties like feeding, washing, drying, ironing swaddling clothes, and a million other things. During the first couple of months, and even though we had a vast amount of help from my mother-in-law and my domestic responsibilities were fairly modest, I had very little time to concentrate on my new job.

Less than three years had passed from the time when I began my work with the lab to the time when I completed the draft of my dissertation. It was a busy and intense time for me, and I was writing the dissertation under my daughter's "vocal accompaniment." Actually, all members of our family were busy. Care of our newborn child consumed a tremendous amount of time, especially if one takes into consideration the conditions we lived in. After Dina's birth we lived with Susanna's parents, sharing two rooms with them. Her parents lived in the larger of two rooms; Susanna, Dina, and I shared the smaller one, which sometimes served us as a kitchen as well. Susanna's mother did not work and tried to help us in every possible way. There was, nevertheless, an endless amount of work for me to do.

At that time we hadn't heard of disposable diapers, and just keeping the child dry meant changing her clothes every half hour, washing them in hot and cold water, hanging them to dry and then ironing them. From the beginning, Susanna could not produce enough milk, so we were forced to shuttle back and forth to special baby kitchens for donated milk or ready-made baby food. This was just a small fraction of our daily family activity. During the day I was in the lab, but in the evenings my research centered on my daughter.

We were young parents, and if Dina was ill it would bring us close to despair, well, if not both of us, me for sure. On top of it all, at the age of two and a half months, Dina was hospitalized with severe dyspepsia. That scary experience added new worries to our troubles with her feeding.

A more frightening incident with Dina happened when she was two or three. I remember Susanna gave her a small piece of orange. After a while, her body began inflating like a rubber pillow. Susanna was scared to death. She called for me, and when I got there and pressed gently on Dina's arm a small indent remained on the spot where I pressed my finger. It was so scary that I panicked. We called the ambulance. The doctor found that it was an allergic reaction caused by the orange. He gave her an anti-allergy injection, and, fortunately, after a while everything returned to normal.

As Dina grew up a little, she developed some new habits. We had no special room for children, and Dina slept in our room. One of her habits was the way she would fall asleep at night. She came up with an annoying habit, one that often drove us crazy. First of all, she wouldn't allow us to close the door between rooms. She wanted to be sure that somebody was in the next room. Trying not to disturb her, we could communicate only by whisper. Secondly, and this was the most frustrating part, she refused to be left alone in the room with the light off, but, if the light was left on, she would only want to play, not sleep.

The only compromise we could make was for someone to be in the room with her when the light was off. I was the only idler in the family it was considered solely my responsibility to be with her in the dark room. Her falling asleep could last for an hour or longer, and during that time, I couldn't watch TV or even read, because the light was off. I couldn't do anything.

Every evening, after Susanna put her in the crib, my duty began. Dina's long journey to sleep usually started with the routine dialogue:

"Daddy, I am afraid."

"What are you afraid of?"

"I am afraid of a wolf and a bear."

"Don't worry, they are not here."

After a short while:

"Daddy, are you going to keep a wolf and a bear out?"

"Of course I am."

This would happen several times while I lay on the bed in the darkness doing nothing but waiting. After twenty or thirty minutes when it seemed that she had fallen asleep, I would hold my breath, ease myself off the bed and, while pressing my body to the floor, try to get out of the room. When half of my body was on the other side of the door a loud cry would tear the silence of our apartment. It was a warning that Dina was still awake and alert and nobody was allowed to cross the border. She was so vigilant that she could be a priceless guard of the highly guarded Soviet borders. For an hour, sometimes more, I would repeat my attempt to leave several more times, before Dina finally fell asleep. Only then would I legally be able to get to my desk and start my evening work.

Dina was twenty months old when we were forced to put her into daycare. It turned out to be stressful for her and a difficult experience for us as well, because she didn't like daycare centers and kindergartens. When we just approached the kindergarten, and she was able to recognize it, she would begin to cry. The most difficult part was to leave her there. The crying was so loud and bitter that we wanted to cry with her, but we had no choice; we both worked and had to go to work.

It was also my responsibility to go with Dina to the closest park, called Kulikovoe Pole, to walk. Like all kids, Dina would get tired from walking, and I would end up carrying her in my arms. Soon she found out the "great truth" that riding was much better than walking and took every opportunity to ask me to carry her even after a short walk. I was told that for her health it wasn't always the right thing to do. In vain, I tried to convince her, but my simple logic just didn't work. She listened to me and seemed to agree with me, but as soon as I finished my educational speech, she wanted me to carry her in my arms.

When my truthful attempts failed, I thought up a tale about a "Big Eagle" that was flying around somewhere. I explained to Dina that if the "Big Eagle" saw me carrying her then the severe bird would peck my arms. She usually stopped crying and agreed to walk only because of the threat of the "Big Eagle." She cared about her parents and wanted nothing to harm me, and I must admit that, for parents, it is a wonderful and warm feeling when you see that your child cares for you. From time to time, updating the situation, she inquired about the "Big Eagle," just to check, and then continued her walk. She never asked me to carry her again.

In general, Dina wasn't a disobedient or spoiled child, but she was an active and fast kid who could do some unexpected things. It was always necessary to keep an eye on her; otherwise she was ready to give us a surprise. I remember back to when we lived with Susanna's parents, sharing their two rooms, my father-in-law liked to take a nap in the daytime on the couch.

One day, he came home from his work later than usual. He had a bottle of fresh buttermilk, opened it, took one sip and put the bottle on his desk near the couch. Then he took his nap, and apparently, being tired, immediately fell asleep. We were at home busy, and Dina was playing somewhere around, running from room to room. Running by the couch, she saw Grandpa sleeping. All of a sudden she grabbed the bottle of buttermilk and began pouring it into Grandpa's open mouth. It could have been a disaster: my poor father-in-law jumped up from the couch, gasping for breath and coughing; he was scared to death. Fortunately, her attempt to feed Grandpa ended without consequence, but from that moment he kept his buttermilk as far away as possible from Dina.

There is no threat of "Big Eagle"

Eighteen

The First Scar

1968

From her birth Dina was a beautiful child with blond hair like a doll. Everybody paid attention to her and tried to play with her. As a little baby she looked fragile, and this constantly kept me alert. I was especially worried when something harmful happened to her. I still have a scar on my forehead that I call a "sign of parents' love." The scar reminds me of one "comedy drama" episode. However, at that time it was rather drama and wasn't funny at all.

One day, Susanna, Dina and I walked in a park close to our home. For some reason, Dina got capricious; she resisted walking with us, and Susanna pulled her by the arm to make her follow our way. I don't think that the pull was hard, but Dina began to cry complaining that her arm was hurt and she couldn't move it. The arm hung down like a rope, and Dina didn't allow us to touch it. Naturally, I was afraid that Susanna had somehow dislocated her arm. I say "naturally" because I was reacting automatically. I took Dina in my arms and told Susanna that we should rush to emergency. We started to look for a taxi.

Susanna was running ahead of me, and I followed her with Dina in my arms. As we were crossing the street, I stumbled over the curb and began falling down. Susanna sensed that something was going wrong with me and turned around to support me. She was a little too late. I couldn't stop and, continuing to fall, hit her glasses with my forehead. Fortunately, colliding with Susanna stopped me from falling down on the ground. On the other hand, the impact had a double "side effect." The collision was so hard that it broke Susanna's eyeglasses into many tiny fragments. Some of the fragments went into her eyes and she wasn't able to open them. I managed to warn Susanna that she mustn't even try to open her eyes or clean them. A large fragment from her eyeglasses cut a blood vessel on my forehead, and blood flowed into both my eyes. Now, we were both blind.

Apparently it was a colorful picture. I kept Dina in my hands; blood was dripping from my forehead, and my face and shirt were covered with blood. Neither Susanna nor I could open our eyes; we weren't able to see anything and stood helplessly in the middle of the street, not knowing in which direction to go. Finally, someone helped us to cross the street, and then stopped a taxi that rushed us to the closest emergency room.

The doctor didn't know whom to help first. I was worried about Susanna's eyes so he started with her and carefully cleaned her eyes. Finishing with Susanna, he treated me by putting a patch on my forehead. After we regained the ability to see and speak, we told the doctor what our main concern was, explaining to him what had happened to Dina's left arm. He tried to examine her arm, but she began crying again and didn't allow him to touch the arm and check it.

He looked at Dina's arm not touching it, thought for a while then took off his watch and asked Dina, "Do you want this watch?" Of course, she wanted it. She tried to grab it with her right hand, but the doctor said, "No, if you want the watch take it with the other hand." The watch was so nice and attractive that Dina raised her left hand and grabbed the watch! Thus, Dina's healing was over; I got a patch on my forehead; Susanna was able to open her eyes. All three of us were happy and free to go.

Nineteen

Better Than Mountains

1969 to 1978

I worked for a research lab and for a long time had no vacation. I liked my work and worked hard. Sometimes I was so tired and exhausted that I felt the necessity to relax or take a little rest, but I didn't know how to do it. I asked my coworkers and other people and, finally, got an idea.

One of my friends, who I had known for years, had experience in mountain tourism. He often described his adventures when he was hiking in the Caucasus, and his stories inspired me to try such "active rest." I found a companion: my friend Yura Botuk expressed a desire to join me. We both had no previous experience in mountain hiking and did not realize many things. After speaking with some knowledgeable people who had that experience, we traced a route, found the necessary though not always perfect equipment, and were ready to conquer the mountain peaks.

Because of our primitive outfit, cotton sleeping bags, canvas tent, alcohol-Primus (stove) etc. and five-day food reserve, our backpacks were bulky and heavy, weighing over forty pounds each. We resembled camels but felt like pioneers and didn't pay much attention to how we looked. I remember my mom's reaction. She was so worried about my trip that she began crying when she saw the huge backpack on my back.

I also remember a conversation. We had already gone to Georgia and were in a local railway station waiting for a bus. Two Georgians approached us. They looked at our backpacks and asked where we were going with such big bags and wondered how much our employer had paid us for the job. When we explained to them that we were doing it for pleasure, they shrugged, saying with astonishment, "Are you guys crazy?"

We started our route by ourselves. At the first camp where we stopped for an overnight rest, we got acquainted with a group of mountain tourists. They had a guide who was a Georgian resident. He lived in the area and knew the Caucasus Mountains like his backyard. All heavy tourist equipment which belonged to his group was loaded on a not big but hardy donkey. With the guide's permission, we joined the group; however, we were supposed to carry our backpacks ourselves. The next morning, after a couple of hours of walking, we knew exactly what the donkey felt and were full of sympathy for the poor animal.

The core of that route was a mountain pass, which was located at a relatively high elevation. For us, untrained adventurers accustomed mostly to seat work, the trip was difficult but rewarding. My legs and back ached, but it was insignificant compared to what I experienced. I was impressed by the ringing silence of the mountains and its severe beauty. I liked the icy-cold, roaring, fast rivers and creeks, and many natural mineral springs of tasty carbonated water, and I drank it like a horse. After this first trip I fell in love with the mountains. Since then, for many consecutive summers, I used to organize a group of three to five of my friends and colleagues, plan a tour in a new region, and go to the mountains. Our homecomings were always joyful, but sometimes they ended with some hilarious incidents.

The first several years of her life, Dina was a "daddy's girl." Of course, her attachment to me filled my heart with great pleasure, but on the other hand, it created a serious problem for me when I had to go anywhere, even on a business trip. Each time when she saw me leaving, she began to cry. It was impossible to give her a good-bye kiss without upsetting her. Not wishing to make her cry, I had to leave secretly, and as soon as I came back from any of my trips, I looked forward to seeing my women, and meetings with Dina were full of joy and kisses. Surprisingly, my meeting with her after my first mountain trip appeared to be an unexpected exception.

During the trip, I did not shave, and my beard grew out. My teammates joked that I looked like a Viking. Coming home, I joined Susanna to pick up Dina from the kindergarten. When Dina saw me with a beard and mustache, she couldn't recognize me and began to cry. It took a long while to calm her down. Later on, Dina grew accustomed to my "bearded" appearance and didn't mind it. I kept the beard after one of my succeeding trips and wore it for many years.

Of course, all people pay attention when one of their coworkers changes his appearance. When I came to the institute with the beard, most of my colleagues reacted to my appearance with jokes. I expected the same from all others, but someone (he posed as a "big potato") looked at my beard and said, "Shave it. You work in an educational institute, and you show a bad example to your students."

I got angry. "A bad example to my students? What is your problem? It isn't your business," I thought. Nevertheless, I restrained myself and said smiling, "Listen, my friend. Tell me, what is better: to be stupid or bald?" He looked at me, puzzled, not knowing what to say (He was absolutely bald). "To be stupid is better," I continued. "And do you know why? Stupidity isn't so visible." It was the end of the discussion.

After my first trip to the Caucasus, the mountains enchanted me. Working in an educational institute, I easily could get a vacation in the summer time, and having such opportunity, I did not even want to think of going anywhere else. It was always an adventure, a lot of fun and joy. We usually came home a little tired but happy. Each route was different, and each trip had had something new and exiting. Usually, before returning home, the final part of all trips was resting one to three days on the sea beaches. As a rule, that part was without adventures.

I also took part on a kayak trip, which was a new experience for me, and although it was exciting and full of bright impressions, I remained loyal to mountaineering. As before, I was longing to go to the mountains, because I liked mountain trips better than anything else. As the Russian bard Vladimir Vysotzkiy used to sing, "Better than mountains could be only mountains where you hadn't been before." Many years have passed since I was on those wonderful trips, but my memory still retains the different events and episodes from those days. The trips occurred in different years; I didn't stick to exact chronological order in the description, but what all these episodes have in common is that they happened in the Caucasus Mountains.

Every year I planned a new route. Some of the trips were easier; some were more difficult, but all of them required certain training (which I never had) and reasonable caution. I wouldn't consider them risky or dangerous like mountain climber's routes; nevertheless, all of them, without a doubt, did contain elements of visible or hidden risk.

It was in the middle of the day that we found ourselves on top of a deep and steep gorge—it was so steep that it was impossible to keep our feet on the slope. If one were to fall, he would slip down to the bottom, unable to grasp anything in order to prevent himself from falling. The upper part of the gorge, approximately forty to fifty yards from the edge, was partly grassy and partly just bare land, and the lower part of it was almost a vertical cliff, fifteen to twenty yards deep. A rapid, not too wide mountain river with many large rocks throughout ran at the bottom of the gorge. Four or five yards below the gorge edge, a small path led to the plateau where we were heading. Our team was following the path when we saw a creek that crossed the path and partially washed it out. The creek at the intersection with the path was a little wider than one yard.

Secured by a rope, one of my teammates crossed the stream first and descended several yards below to secure the rest of us. Second teammate successfully crossed the stream, stepping on a small rock in the middle of the stream. I was third, and stepped on the same rock as he did. Apparently, stepping over the creek, my mate had moved the rock, and it came loose, but I didn't see that. As a result, I lost my foothold and began to fall down—it was a free fall. I was falling an unreachable distance from the hiker who crossed the stream first. In a split second he made the only right decision, which I believe saved my life: holding the handle of an ice axe in his right hand, he quickly stuck it just under my foot and stopped me from sliding any farther. It all happened so fast that I had no time to get scared. I saw my teammates pale as they watched. Later, discussing the situation, they admitted that nobody had a shadow of a doubt in their minds that if my rescuer hadn't stopped my fall, it probably would have been my last trip. After coming home, I kept silent about what had happened to me, not wishing my family to worry whenever I went to the mountains.

Steep slopes always have some hidden danger. I remember one more incident we had with a slope, though this incident wasn't as dramatic as the previous one. In spite of the fact that the adventure brought us some pain in the buttocks (literally), the situation was really funny and made us laugh.

As it is well known, sometimes a descent can be more difficult than a climb. We had a long descent from the mountains; our legs were aching badly from the load, and our knees were trembling. Finally, we approached a grassy steep slope, which didn't seem too long; however, it was too steep to walk on. As we estimated it would take a long time and an additional couple of miles to walk around it and, wishing to save us a walk, we inspected the grass. It seemed long and soft, and to make our way down shorter and quicker, we decided to slide down, using our own buttocks as a sled. For better protection we spread our waterproof jackets under our "sleds."

Only in the middle of our way down, we understood what a serious mistake we had made; we miscalculated the safety of the grass. Soft didn't mean safe—the grass appeared to be full of plants and debris and had a lot of prickles and long thorns. We realized too late what we had done, but it was already impossible to stop: we were sliding down fast. All of us came down with buttocks that looked like a pair of hedgehogs. Regardless of how we tried to coil up or twist our bodies, self-treatment wasn't effective. Finally, we split up into two teams, pulled down our trousers and pants, and taking suitable postures, began to pull out the thorns and splinters one by one, helping each other.

Some of the thorns were so small that it took a lot of effort and inventiveness to get them out. I can only imagine what an unforgettable picture it would have been for anybody who might have watched us from aside, but at such a dramatic moment nobody cared to think about how they looked. We were much too busy with our buttocks to think or take pictures. Speaking about an "unforgettable picture," I have to say that when people get into unusual circumstances they often ignore many, if not all, conventionalities, which they hold sacred or at least are strictly consistent with their everyday life.

We were ascending Elbrus, and our goal was to get to a mountain tourist shelter, called "Priyut 11," which was located at an elevation of 4,200 meters (approximately 14,000 feet). As usual, our trip took place in the middle of summer, and at the beginning of the route, the weather was so hot and the air was so dry that the sweat on our faces evaporated instantly, leaving a thick layer of salt on all of our cheeks. We tried to scrape off the salt with our hands, but it didn't bring much relief.

For the next couple of days as we were ascending, the weather was changing and the temperature was dropping. Large spots of snow began to appear here and there. The temperature had already dropped below zero Celsius when unexpectedly the rain started. We had some waterproof protection, like plastic raincoats, but they were in our backpacks, and while we tried to reach them, we got soaked to the skin. When we finally got our raincoats, they appeared to be useless. Besides, they were long and so inconvenient that it made it impossible to continue the ascent, and, finally, we put them back into the backpacks.

Soon the situation had changed from bad to worse: our faces, hands, and legs were covered with a crust of ice; our clothes became icy, and it was more and more difficult to go on. At the end of the day, with the great difficulties, we reached some intermediate shelter. It was a small wooden hut, with one large room and a heating furnace or a stove in it. Entering the room, we saw many young male and female tourists, standing around the stove or sitting on beds. Some of them were naked as newborns, though nobody paid much attention to that. They invited us to a warm spot near the stove and offered us a special place where we could dry our clothes. None of us could find anything dry in our backpacks, and after not much hesitation we joined the group of nudists. I still remember how much effort it cost me to get undressed and "join the club." I saw many others like us; they didn't feel naked and were able to speak with each other as if they were dressed in tuxedos...

Each trip, even a difficult one, had something interesting or funny. Usually, when we went to the mountains, we had a limited supply of emergency food, because we didn't expect to be out of a populated area for more than four or five days. The episode I am going to write about now happened at the end of one of our passages through the mountains. We were two more walking days from the closest shelter when we found a suitable spot in a wooded area and set up a tent. In our previous trips to the Caucasus Mountains, none of us had ever met bears, deer, or other big animals. Having had such great experience, we had nothing to be afraid of and hid the remainder of our emergency food supply (some dry food and cans) under the tent, near the entrance.

In the early morning, grunting noises and some soft pounding on the tent awakened our "camp." When we crawled out, we saw a family or two of wild pigs. They were skinny and hairy like dogs and they also were hungry like dogs (If they weren't pigs I would have said "hungry as pigs"). I had never seen wild pigs before, and watched with great interest how these swinish families were eating everything they could get. We tried to frighten them away, but it was useless: they were running off and coming back, not wishing to give up. Finally, we forced them to get out and were able to assess the damages they had done to our camp. Of course, all the dry food was completely gone along with wrappings and covers, and all the canned food was chewed up and had many holes from the pigs' teeth. Apparently they found several of our wool socks (those, I guess, which had a more attractive odor) along with a pair of washed pants to be delicious and ate them as well. Fortunately, we had some spare socks, but we were left without food, because the food in the cans wasn't edible at all and had to be dumped.

So, we quickened our steps, hoping to reach a tourist center sooner and to shorten the "starving" time. At the end of the next day, we happened to see a small meadow where two or three guys were cleaning their campsite. We approached them, told them about the pigs' invasion, and asked if they had some food that they could share with us. It turned out that they were with a group, and that the group had already gone away, leaving a few duty mates to clean the site. I can imagine what they read on our faces when one of them laughingly said, "Stop dying, guys. We have some leftovers to offer you." And they offered us a two-gallon bucket full of liquid, like milk, semolina kasha, and a bucket with cold unsweetened cocoa. The kasha wasn't just a kasha— it was manna from heaven for us.

When we got the food we discovered that one more test was waiting for us: we couldn't find our spoons. Apparently, we had left them somewhere or had thrown them away accidentally while cleaning the pigs' mess. Our "rescuers" had only teaspoons to offer, nevertheless it didn't take more than several minutes for the four of us to empty the bucket, working only with teaspoons. Unfortunately, there weren't officials who could register our "eating" achievement; otherwise, we certainly would have been qualified for the Guinness Book of World Records.

Caucasus Mountains
Solomon (center) with friends

Twenty

How Can He Be a Boss?

1969 to 1978

As a rule, any Caucasus Mountain trips began at a tourist center, which was commonly located near a foot of the mountain. The "organized" tourists (i.e. those who had bought tour packages in advance) were transported to the centers by trucks equipped with benches for passengers, and then the journey from the center to a trailhead took approximately three to four hours.

The roads to the centers went along mountain gorges; all those serpentine roads were unpaved, narrow even for one car and risky. The slightest driver's carelessness and a car or a truck would fall down into a gorge, often with deadly consequences. There was a Caucasus tradition to place a memorial post at the places where deadly accidents had occurred. Tourists called those memorial posts "nesting boxes," and sometimes people put in them a bottle of wine and a glass in case somebody, according to Georgian tradition, would like to drink to the memory of the deceased. The local people said that usually several new "nesting boxes" appeared every tourist season.

On one of our trips, we asked a truck driver's permission to join the group of organized tourists he was going to drive to the center. The driver, a local Georgian with a big moustache, didn't mind, especially when he heard about a separate payment, and pointed to the last bench on his truck. After half an hour of driving, he made a stop near a wooden house at the side of the road and went into the house. Several minutes later two Georgians came out from the house and approached the truck. One of them, with a gloomy face, looked at the people in the truck and asked threateningly, "Who is the boss?" I was the organizer of our trip and my friends, not fully understanding what was going on, pointed at me for some reason, though certainly I wasn't the boss. The gloomy man nodded in my direction, and briefly said, as ordered, "Follow me," and both men went to the house. I ought to confess that such an invitation made me a little worried: I didn't know what to expect.

When we entered the house, I saw our driver and one more Georgian sitting at the dining table in the middle of the room. I also saw several glasses on the table, two large vessels with some liquid, and a couple of plates with colorful pieces of unfamiliar vegetables on them. By the smell coming from the vessels, one could recognize Georgian "chacha," the strong alcohol drink commonly made from grape or mulberry fruits. Regular chacha was weaker than pure alcohol, but much stronger than regular Russian vodka.

The driver filled full glasses of the drink for everybody, not forgetting to pour one for himself as well. Seeing the glass filled with chacha that they moved toward me, I energetically shook my head: I hated even the smell of it. The gloomy man fiercely looked at me, pointed at the glass, and didn't take his eyes off mine until I drank it to the bottom. When I finished, he approvingly nodded and gave me a piece of something from the plate. I tried that "something" and felt like I had put a lit torch in my mouth that already was burning after the chacha. The men laughed, and someone poured mineral water in my glass. It helped a little. I didn't have enough time to ventilate and cool down my mouth when the gloomy man filled my glass again and briefly ordered, "Drink!" His entire appearance made it clear that resistance was futile. I forced myself to swallow some more, and more… and I missed the moment when I plunged into darkness.

The rest of the story I learned from my friends. After I entered the house, they waited for twenty minutes or so and became more and more worried. They had already decided to look inside the house to find out what was going on when the driver and two men appeared at the door, carrying me in their arms. They approached the truck and put me under the bench. One of them, looking at my friends, said with great astonishment, "How can he be a boss? He can't drink…" That night I woke up in our tent with a severe headache, dying of thirst.

Twenty-One

A Couple of Drunkards

1969

Dina started attending a daycare center when she was less than two, and after she grew up a little, we transferred her to a kindergarten. From the beginning, for the next several years when she attended the daycare and then her first kindergarten we had a hard time every day. As with all kids, it was stressful for her to see her parents leaving. In addition, she didn't get along with some of the kindergarten teachers, and it wasn't easy to tell why. Compared to other children, she was an energetic and active child, and perhaps, that could have been a part of the problem. On the other hand, the main reason for her rebellious behavior could have been the staff's mistakes: they always were too severe, harsh, and pushy with kids, making no adjustments for children's individual personalities.

In fact, the problem was considerably mitigated, I would say disappeared, after our neighbor who we knew many years and were very friendly, admitted Dina to the kindergarten where she worked.

She and her husband were simple and good people. She knew Dina from her birth and loved her. Besides, she and her staff had a much better approach to children, and, in general, were gentle and patient with kids.

Dina's kindergarten was located a couple of blocks from our home, no more than four or five minutes of walking distance. Continually busy at our work, we were often late from work to pick Dina up. In such cases, somebody from neighbors, who also worked there, frequently took her home. Dina loved when neighbors took her home. She called them "aunts" and "uncles."

Once I came to the kindergarten to take Dina and was told that a neighbor had already picked her up. I went home, looking for Dina, and neither Dina nor the neighbor was at home. "Okay," I thought, "apparently they will come soon." After an hour or so, I began worrying, and what made things worse, I did not know where to look for them. Many times I went back and forth from home to the kindergarten, hoping to meet them. I almost panicked when at last they came.

Both of them were happy and joyful as if nothing happened. Dina had a smile on her face from ear to ear, and she was pleased to inform us that she was with the uncle neighbor, and they had a great time. The uncle had gotten a big mug of beer for himself, and a small mug of beer for Dina. At the beginning, she explained to us, the beer was a little bitter, but she tried it again and liked it better, and, generally, life was nice and wonderful. We didn't know what to say. Fortunately, except for sleeping deeply that night and a couple of extra trips to the bathroom, there were no other consequences.

Twenty-Two

Dina's Education

1969 to 1974

Dina was a cute, lively and capable child with a quick mind and inexhaustible energy. It wasn't surprising that we considered her the smartest kid, although I realize that being a parent it is hard to be absolutely objective when you are speaking about your children. She had a beautiful appearance and was our first child, and that all together made her adorable. Whenever I had a chance I tried to teach her everything I believed to be useful. I taught her letters, words, and how to put together words and read them; I showed her numbers and some simple arithmetic, and I did that, turning everything into a game. I read a lot of children's books to her, and we played children's games. I also taught her drawing and painting. My approach worked nicely, and she was developing fairly well.

When she was five, I began more systematic teaching, hoping that if she could learn to read fluently enough, she would be able to read books herself. Maybe it sounds selfish, but I have to confess, Susanna and I hoped that it would release some time for us. Secondly, I strongly believed (and continue to believe) in self-education. Anyway, I began methodical and regular tutoring, but at that time I had no easy success. My approach didn't work as well as it did the first time. First of all, Dina didn't like reading for too long; she didn't like to make an effort, and fiercely resisted any homework. Of course, it was a cause for arguments and tears. In addition, after a while, she more and more frequently read words, replacing the beginnings and ends. It made me upset, because I thought that she did it intentionally, just for fun and this habit drove me crazy. At that time, I didn't know that such things happened with children, and doctors even have a special term for such conditions, but I learned that much later.

So, I continued my educational "sorrow," being sure that when Dina overcame initial difficulties and read better, she would love to read. Fortunately, it was the case: her "syllables rearrangement" finally disappeared, and she enjoyed reading, but it took much more time than I expected.

Thus, it wasn't a total failure: I did gain some useful teaching experience. One more thing I would like to add: to my pride, while I sharpened my educational skills, I made a discovery, so to speak, a "reading substitute." We bought many wonderful children's long-playing records like children's operas, musical and non-musical tales, and some children's plays. I showed Dina how to operate the record player, and she could listen to these records for hours. I, myself, when I had a chance, listened to all of them with pleasure.

Dina grew up and something new popped up. She always was a good student, and her grades were high. She was a capable kid and had no difficulty in studies, but there was one school problem we weren't able to solve even for a while. It was chatter during classes. She chatted with her classmates without breaks. Her "verbal activity" interrupted lessons and irritated teachers. Dina's class supervisor used to write down in the children's diaries (the pupil's personal grade books) her observation and comments about their behavior. For many years, up to our emigration, I kept Dina's school diary as a memory of the teachers' self-sacrificing fight for students' discipline in classrooms. Written with red ink, it was a crescendo of desperate cries, and the same pattern recurred every week. Monday: "Parents, please pay attention, Dina chats during classes." Tuesday: "Dina again was chatting all day long!" Wednesday: "Dina still continues to chat!!" Thursday: "Please, take care, Dina is chatting again and again!!!" Friday: "I am exhausted! Parents, please come to the school ASAP." (By the way, some similar, but, maybe not so dramatic "screams," we read later in Vova's personal grade book.)

Of course, we spoke with Dina many times. Of course, she always had plenty of excuses, like: it was somebody else who spoke with her first, and she just had to answer, or she couldn't hear the teacher's explanation and was forced to ask her classmate. There was nothing we could do about it; we were exhausted as well. Ironically, I recall how I taught her to walk and to speak when she was a toddler. Regarding that matter, somebody wise noticed correctly, "We are teaching children to walk and to speak in order to force them later on to sit and keep their mouths shut."

Twenty-Three

Abandoned

1971

It was in 1971. I had already known that my department, including the lab where I worked, had to be transferred to the Polytechnic Institute. It was summer—a vacation time, and I planned to spend it for recreational purposes or something interesting.

I learned that two or three hikers were preparing to go on an interesting trip. They were going by kayaks downstream on the small northern River Vaymuga. (Vaymuga feeds the big Russian river called the North Dvina.) One of their group-mates invited me to join them. The Vaymuga River was neither a wide nor very fast river, but it had several rapids and small waterfalls, though it was without big rocks and not too dangerous. There were also one or two shallow places, where it was necessary to carry the kayaks by hand or on our backs like backpacks. I had no experience in kayaking before, but the trip promised to be interesting, and without much hesitation I made up my mind to go.

The group included five men and one woman. Four of us were approximately the same age and the fifth was a hunter who was much older than we. Our team chief was a reliable and experienced traveler.

I don't remember who had invited that "man with a rifle" to join us. It seemed that our chief had done it. If indeed it was he, I have no idea where he found the guy and what the rationale of this invitation was. Apparently, he thought that the hunter, having good experience in hunting, would help us in case there was a shortage of food, since we were going to sparsely populated places, or it might be he just invited him for fun.

The trip wasn't always easy. Sometimes we had a hard time, and it wasn't necessarily physical difficulties or dangerous situations. Although we were prepared thoroughly and even had a special mesh protection which beekeepers usually use for bees, we suffered a lot from mosquitoes. These fierce animals managed to bite us through thick tourist ammunition. We also had different mosquito-repellent ointments, but that odorous stuff seemed to attract them even more. I suspect they liked the smell of the ointment and just waited for us to apply it. In the dusk, in the early evening, and frequently in the daytime, any trip to the coast or forest for natural needs was a true torture. Just the thought that it would be necessary to bare even a tiny fraction of our body was unbearable. Many times, damning our own body, we postponed our urgent travels to the coast or forest up to the point when each additional second of delay could lead to disastrous consequences. I was suffering a lot, shrinking each time when I heard the hateful familiar sound. Only near the end of the trip I did gain some friendship, rather immunity, from those flying bulls.

In hindsight, long after my mosquito wounds have healed, I can say that, in general, the trip was indeed interesting and enjoyable. Wild Northern Nature impressed me with its real beauty. We didn't want our hunter to hunt, so nobody hunted; we only permitted ourselves to fish. Our fisherman treated us with fresh and tasty river fish quite often. The whole team shared one small tent, being packed in it like sardines. At night when the tent was unfolded and ready for sleeping, two of us had to slip inside the tent, tighten the entry and windows, and, after flashing the flashlights, hunt for mosquitoes. We went to sleep only when the last one was killed. Literally, the last one. Otherwise, it would be a sleepless night. Imagine for a moment: you desperately want to sleep, and hear the sound of a mosquito, and you are thinking about when and where it is going to land. On your face or somebody else's? Then, you hear a loud slap, and a second or two later, the same mosquito sound reminds you that you can be the next victim. Now try to sleep!

Our expectations regarding the hunter didn't come true: he turned out to be a poor team player. Instead of doing something useful, he drove us crazy with his idiotic discussions whether "duck stood on wing" or not. This mysterious expression was a hunter's slang, which meant that baby birds learned to fly. Wishing to show what a great hunter he was, he used this funny expression to the point and beside the point, but more frequently, it was absolutely out of place. His stupid and doubtful hunting stories irritated us. They were classic illustrations of the so-called "hunters' tales." However, his stupid stories and birds' stuff were just half the trouble—he did not want to take part in food preparation, dish washing, cleaning the site before leaving, etc. He was a bad partner in kayaking as well, and soon all of us were reluctant to share a kayak with him. The last straw was his refusal to maintain his kayak. Finally, in the middle of the trip, after discussion with us, our chief suggested to him that he leave us. When we reached the first village, he left.

The River Vaymuga runs mostly through unpopulated areas. On our way downstream, we passed just a couple of villages. They were typical northern villages with dusty and bumpy dirt roads, inhabited by mostly aged men and women living in old blackened and distorted log houses. There was nothing unusual in such a picture. But one thing we saw struck me; I had never seen anything like it before. It was an abandoned village, and I felt like we had seen a real ghost town.

At first we didn't recognize that the village was abandoned and turned our heads around hoping to see somebody alive. We wandered through it and saw streets and houses, but we did not see anybody. We saw no animals; we didn't hear barking dogs or the squeak of wells. There were no sounds at all. Suddenly I saw a school. It was in the middle of a street with residential houses and surrounded by a wooden fence. The school building was empty, and its windows were broken and nailed down by crossed boards. Some of the houses had broken widows, and some were with nailed shutters. We found the house where the village government offices were located when the village was alive. "Was alive" are the right words; now it was a dead place. Uneasy, sad and disturbing feelings wrapped us all.

Unexpectedly, we saw thin smoke coming from the chimney of one of those lifeless houses. We knocked on the door and went in. We found two old women inside. One of them was much older than other. I believe she was over eighty or even ninety. The woman was lying on the bed, covered with a dirty, ragged blanket. As we learned later, the other woman, in her late sixties or seventies, was a daughter of the older one. She was sitting at the table, drinking something from a cup that she held with both hands.

They told us that the village was really abandoned. They would like to leave also, but they were lonely and had no place to go. Year after year, youngsters were leaving the village and going to towns and cities where they could find a job or better life. The old people gradually died out. Those two old women were the "last Mohicans" in the village. They told us that for a couple of months in the wintertime they were given shelter by their former neighbor who moved to live with her son in a small town one hundred miles away. Seeing those old, lonely, and helpless women, I wanted to cry. Unfortunately, there was nothing we could do to help them. We went back to our kayaks and brought them two thirds of the food supply that we had and left the village.

The rest of the journey we completed without any further adventures. Our "kayak convoy" sailed up to the North Dvina River to the city of Archangelsk, an old Russian northern city. Time hadn't changed the city significantly; we saw a lot of old, even ancient, buildings. After a short stop, we got on the train and went back to Odessa.

Twenty-Four

My Surgery

1971

Although some things in our lives develop gradually, as a rule, we discover them all of a sudden. That's exactly what happened to me. I was accustomed to wearing a necktie practically every day because it was like a dress code for educational and professional organizations in the Soviet Union. One day, buttoning the collar of my shirt before putting on a tie, I felt some discomfort. I touched my neck, and under the Adam's apple, I found something like a round ball which was an inch-size in diameter. Usually, the ball wasn't seen or felt unless I spoke or ate, and it was palpable only when I made a swallowing motion. I did not consider myself an expert in anatomy but understood that it was something abnormal. I still didn't pay much attention to it and didn't care to tell anybody about my "discovery." After a while, when I asked Susanna to move the collar button and explained to her why it was necessary, she got alarmed and convinced me to visit a doctor. I did it. The doctor appeared to be an old gentleman who previously was a practicing surgeon. After a short examination he told me that the "ball" was a benign thyroidal node and there was nothing to worry about. Nevertheless, Susanna wanted a second opinion.

The second opinion we got from Kishinev doctors, Susanna's relatives who at that time lived in the city of Kishinev, which was Moldova's capital and located approximately 180 kilometers from Odessa. The relatives, Lyova, a radiologist, and Fira Fishov, a pediatrician, were both well-known doctors in Kishinev. They used to give us advice regarding our children and our various medical problems. We were frequent guests in Kishinev, coming for family celebrations, gatherings, and for shopping as well, because as a capital, Kishinev had probably a much better supply of everything than Odessa.

It happened that we were in Kishinev for some regular celebration, and Susanna took the opportunity to tell Lyova what I had discovered on my throat. Lyova examined me and suggested that we consult with a couple of his colleagues: one was an experienced surgeon, and the other was a therapist. Both of them confirmed that I had a thyroidal knob, which is generally benign and more common for women than for men, the fact which didn't make me any happier. They also mentioned that there were alarming statistical data, which showed that it was safer to have the node removed. In some cases it could enlarge and become the cause of serious problems or, as they expressed, it was like living on a powder keg. Both doctors advised me to consider surgery to remove it, and not to wait until it became a time bomb. After deliberating for not long I decided to follow their recommendations. But first of all it was necessary to decide who, where, and when it would be done.

I had a choice: I could have the operation in Kishinev (the Kishinev doctors offered their help) or in Odessa. Both options had some advantages and disadvantages. When we were back in Odessa, we consulted with some local doctors and discussed their availability. Finally, I chose to have a surgery in Odessa by the surgeon who could schedule the surgery within the next two weeks. He had good references, was recommended to us as a reliable surgeon, and after meeting with him, I felt comfortable with my choice. One more question that I had to resolve was the date of the surgery.

A couple of months each year my mother lived with my brother, Roma, in Leningrad, but for most of the year she preferred to live with us. As with any person in poor health, she was sensitive and vulnerable to any bad news or troubles, and, naturally, we tried to protect her from unnecessary negative emotions. For those reasons I developed the habit of never mentioning my problems in her presence, especially health problems, and now I decided to keep my forthcoming operation from her. I was sure that she would notice my absence for the surgery; therefore, I thought up a tale of having to go to a collective farm as a supervisor of students' agricultural works that was a common occurrence in the former Soviet Union, and she bought my tale without doubts. Now I could go to the hospital knowing that she wouldn't be adversely affected. According to the hospital rules, I had to come to the hospital two days before the scheduled time, because some preparations and tests were to precede my surgery.

Everything was fine except one routine lab procedure. When the nurses took my blood I fainted and that didn't scare or surprise me: I had experienced spasmodic reactions to pain and some other conditions before. But it concerned the nurses more because they knew some details of the surgery, and my condition could have made it more difficult.

The actual details I learned later from my surgeon. The concern was specifically regarding my ability to tolerate pain. As the doctor explained to me, the thyroid node was located close to the vocal cord, and, manipulating a scalpel so close to the cord, a surgeon had to be careful and constantly control himself by speaking with the patient. For this reason the surgery had to be performed under local anesthesia.

In the operating room, the medics put me on my back, gave me the anesthetic, tied down my arms and legs, and covered my face with a metal grid and a napkin. Nurses covered me with a white sheet, and my belly served as a table for trays with the surgical instruments. The surgery lasted about three hours, and the ability to hear and feel made that experience unusual and even interesting.

During the operation, I heard everything that was going on in the operating room. I heard all the surgeon's and his assistants' conversations and jokes. Like all Odessians I appreciate wit and jokes, but at that time my sense of humor was stuck in my throat in the literal and figurative sense of the word. I guess I was the only person in the operating room who didn't smile.

Periodically, the surgeon asked me questions and waited for my replies. When he cut my tissues, I heard sounds as if somebody was cutting rubber with scissors. It was really an odd experience. Fortunately, I didn't feel any serious pain; however, it was just a big inconvenience to lie flat on my back with covered face and with arms and legs tied to the surgical table not being able to move even slightly. During the surgery, I learned that another patient (my "colleague," so to speak) was also in the operating room. When the surgeon completed the main part of his job on me, his associates began to sew my throat, while he went to the next table and continued with the other patient. Soon I was told that they had already finished repairing me.

After a week, I was released from the hospital and went home. The doctors put a big patch and bandages on my neck that certainly evoked Mother's suspicion. Making a happy face, I told Mom as sincerely as I could that it was nothing to worry about. Certainly, she understood that something wasn't kosher, and whatever it was, it had already been done; I was alive and showed no sign of serious illness. Gradually Mom calmed down; she preferred not to dig further.

Twenty-Five

His Doggy Majesty

1973 to 1987

In 1973, we lived in Susanna's parents' flat. It was considered a good location. Nice sea beaches weren't far away from us—no more than fifteen minutes walking distance. A park with trees and nice green lawns, where many people liked to walk, was located at the front of our building just on the other side of the street.

Dina was nine years old, and we hoped that she would like to walk and play at the park after school. Unfortunately, too few kids her age lived nearby, and she had no friends with whom to play and socialize. Nothing motivated her to get outside the house where she could move, exercise, and spend some time in the fresh air. We considered that to be absolutely necessary, especially for a kid of her age, but she didn't want to go anywhere outside our apartment.

A second concern was her behavior. She had a sensitive nervous system. Quite often she showed an obstinate mood toward some things, didn't behave, and was capricious. We shared our concern with Lilya, an experienced expert and my close friend since our school years. Although Lilya hadn't seen any serious problems, she advised us to adopt a dog. As she told us, that way we "would kill two birds with one stone": First, Dina would have a loyal friend and would take care of the dog, and secondly, they would play and move and run. To be honest, it is necessary to mention that at that time we hadn't fully realized the seriousness of the decision and what kind of commitment we were about to make. We understood it later on. I discussed Lilya's suggestion with Susanna, and we decided that it wouldn't be a bad idea, hoping that the adoption of a dog would bring a lot of good things to Dina's life.

Soon we got the opportunity to adopt a puppy: our friend Julius Goodman had a pet, a miniature pinscher named Quantik. It was a small black dog that looked vicious and aggressive as hell. Sometimes he barked so fiercely that it seemed he would jump out of his skin. He was a real fearless aggressor who used to jump on and try to bite everybody who dared to come into his owners' apartment. After many orders and requests, he would finally calm down, and, growling, would hide under a chair ready to attack again at any time. Any guest's sharp movement could make him angry and aggressive. Nevertheless, he was an incredibly loyal dog. Apparently because of his size nobody took him seriously, and, maybe, because of that he was pretty noisy, though practically harmless.

So, this small monster with a female dog of the same breed fathered three puppies. According to an unwritten rule, the owner of the puppies' father was granted one puppy. Quantik's master knew that we were looking for a puppy, and he offered us one to adopt. Not wishing to have trouble with puppies in the future, we preferred a male dog, and thus, through Quantik we became related to that remarkable family.

It turned out that choosing a name for the puppy wasn't a simple issue. In his young age Julius fell in love with physics and now, honoring his love, called his pet Quantik, which was a tender nickname for "Quantum."

At that time, I worked in the nuclear power field and, following the dog's owner, named our dog Tvel. TVEL is an acronym for the Russian nuclear engineering term "heat-emitting element" or simply "heating element." Now writing about this, a semantic joke comes to mind: In English the acronym would sound like—Hel, which is close to the word "hell" and sometimes (fortunately, not always) accurately reflected Tvel's nature.

Tvel was a cute, small dog, even smaller than his father, Quantik, was. Actually, he was a "pocket" dog. I think it was possible that he could be placed into a coat pocket. Even in his adult age, Tvel was as big as half an ordinary cat, not bigger, nevertheless, his proportions were nice: wide chest, strong masculine legs and a beautiful head with one ear erect sometimes. If you looked at him through binoculars, he looked like a big dog, completely black with a white collar and white socks. The doggy was so cute that he always attracted people's attention. They tried to play with him, but it wasn't safe: he inherited his father's character and regarded himself seriously—he didn't like frivolous treatment.

From the first day, Tvel became a part of our family. When he was a puppy, Susanna used to take care of him as if he was our child. At night he slept in a round paperboard hatbox with high walls, and never ever made a puddle in his paperboard "bedroom." When in the middle of the night he needed to pee, he would whimper, and Susanna would wake up to get him out of the box and then, after the business was done, put him back. However, for two or three months before he grew up, he wasn't embarrassed to make puddles on the floor, and we had a hard time keeping the floor dry.

When members of our family would come home, open the door, and bend down to pet him, he used to jump up to our faces trying to lick our mouths. He was so happy and excited to see us coming that sometimes he wet himself. Tvel was an exceptionally loyal dog, but his loyalty spread only to immediate members of our family, and later on, he recognized close relatives and some friends as well. The amazing thing was that even though he had never seen them before, he showed his friendship and treated them as members of our family from the first time they came in. How this tiny dog managed to recognize who was who is a mystery to me to this day.

It was an interesting observation watching how he treated us differently, according to his feeling of the hierarchy. I was his first priority, the master. Susanna's position in his eyes was a little lower than mine, though he treated both of us as masters. He treated Dina as an equal, like a "sister," whom he allowed to feed him, play and walk with him, but became aggressive and bit her when she (and Susanna as well) tried to put him on a leash: the dog liked his freedom, and the leash was his personal enemy. He didn't try to bite anybody out of the home, just barked fiercely as if he was sending us a message, "You had better keep me away; I can tear the guy to shreds." We kept him on a leash for his own safety, fearing that he could get lost or be too aggressive with others, especially big dogs. On the other hand, if we felt that it was safe enough, we let him run without a leash and enjoy more freedom.

Before we brought Tvel home, we asked Dina if she would like to adopt a dog, and she said she would. Moreover, she became enthusiastic and promised to take good care of him. Routinely, I walked the dog in the morning and evening time. After school hours it was Dina's responsibility, and she usually walked with him in and around Kulikovo Pole Park (square). In order to get to the park it was necessary to cross Sverdlova Street where cars and streetcars were running. Dina had detailed instructions how and where to cross the street. She also had a strict instruction to always keep Tvel on a leash, and usually, she followed the instructions.

One day when Dina went for a walk with Tvel and we were at home, they returned with a man we had never seen before. Immediately we felt that something wrong had occurred. The man was a driver for a Party boss—he was visibly scared. We learned what had happened from his and Dina's explanation.

After a long walk Dina was heading home. Halfway home she decided to give Tvel some freedom and unhooked the leash from the collar. Everything seemed okay. They approached a side street where cars weren't too frequent. Following our instructions, Dina was going to buckle the leash again, but suddenly Tvel saw a dog across the street. I should mention that when Tvel saw any dog he became uncontrollable. Surprisingly enough, his reaction to cats was much calmer. So he saw a dog and with a hysteric bark dashed across the street; desperately yelling, Dina followed him. It was that unlucky moment when a car was going along the street. The driver of the car, seeing Tvel, slammed on the brakes. The screaming breaks scared Tvel, and he stopped in the middle of the road. In vain Dina tried to

109

catch him. Somehow the driver managed to stop the car just slightly hitting her. It was the greatest luck that she didn't get hurt. After the accident Dina got the strongest instruction to never ever walk with Tvel without a leash again.

Thus, Tvel helped us to solve (unfortunately only for a while) some of Dina's problems. She walked with him once a day, fed him, and more or less took care of him; sadly, the honeymoon didn't last long. Her initial enthusiasm faded sooner than we expected. We couldn't allow our responsibility to diminish and we silently picked up our additional duties. We didn't have a choice. Thus, for us adults, the story with the dog adoption ended having one more child to worry about.

In the beginning we all had a good deal of fun with the puppy, and only later did we realize how much responsibility we had brought into our family. He lived for many years, causing a lot of problems and troubles for us. On the other hand, he brought plenty of positive emotions in our life. The dog taught us humanity. Despite all unavoidable difficulties, it was a good experience for our children and for us as well.

Dina with Tvel
Tvel became a part of our family

Twenty-Six

One Child Is Too Few

1974 to 1975

Several years after my daughter Dina's birth, when people asked me why we had only one child I usually laughed saying that certainly one child was too few, but two children were too many, and I didn't know how to solve the puzzle. Of course, it was a joke. They say that behind each joke there is a fraction of truth, but behind my joke was more than that. For us it wasn't only a matter of income, which, by the way, was quite modest; other factors also came into play. Our living conditions were less than modest: our family of three still lived in two rooms in a communal apartment which we shared with three other families or a total of twelve persons (sometimes even more). The families were growing; however, the facilities remained the same: one bathroom, one single toilet, and one tiny kitchen for all the residents, not much larger than the toilet. Our prospects for getting something even slightly better than what we had were slim, at least, in the foreseeable future.

Our parents understood the situation and behaved delicately in the matter of trying not to interfere in our family business. Nevertheless, after a while I started noticing signs of their impatience and concern. Often it was by kinds of indirect talk or hints like those that my mother-in-law used to mention, ostensibly as an aside. As if by accident she would say, "You know, Dina is already grown up, so I could help you with another one." I am not sure if Susanna and her mother were more straightforward and frank between them, but, at least, in my presence there were only "roundabout maneuverings" from her mother.

To tell the truth, I was thinking about having a second child. I hoped that a right time would come, though clearly understanding that waiting for the right and proper time could go on forever. One could ask, "What time is the right time?" I didn't know how to determine exactly the right time, but my philosophy was that it was better not to have children than to have them and not to be able to provide the necessary support. If having a child seems like a natural thing, the number of children is frequently a matter of serious considerations. I couldn't stop thinking about our responsibility and the many other circumstances related to the birth of a child.

For those who don't like children, one child is too many or is a "collateral necessity," but for those who love children one child isn't a family yet. Besides, from the standpoint of children, having siblings is a great joy for many. One more relevant observation of child psychologists concerning siblings is that an only child in a family frequently becomes selfish and self-focusing.

Now, when I look back and think about the times when we just began our parenthood some thoughts come into my mind. I remember my feelings when Dina and Vova were born. I remember them in the first days of their lives. When I saw a newborn child, this diminutive body with a small head, tiny hands and legs, miniature fingers and toes, it was impossible for me to get rid of a sense that it was a miracle. And indeed it was a miracle. Our neighbor, a girl of fifteen, touchingly expressed that feeling when she first saw little Vova. She looked at him with admiration and exclaimed, "What a little miracle you are!"

Life is a priceless gift for human beings. However, to give birth doesn't mean to give life in a full sense of the word. The birth is only the beginning and a long and difficult way lies ahead. Thousands of sleepless nights, years of endless worries and troubles, emotional roller coasters, and constant sacrifices are just a part of the way. And the way is as long as the parents' life. What children don't understand frequently is that regardless of their age they always remain children to their parents. Their misfortune is the parents' pain; their joy and success are parents' joy and pride. All parents know that there couldn't be a bigger reward than their children's love and nothing could be bitterer than the lack of their love or even worse—their ingratitude. Where does it all come from? Who knows? I saw somewhat abusive families with children who despite rough treatment dearly loved their parents. I saw loving and caring families with selfish children. Maybe everything I thought sounded obvious, but it was the truth.

All parents usually have high hopes for their children. They want their children to inherit their best qualities and much more. Alas, not everything is in our hands. I heard a joke in which a beautiful but not too smart actress told a famous English playwright, who maybe wasn't a handsome man but had a well-deserved reputation as a clever and witty person, "I want to have a child with you."

"Why?" the writer asked.

"I wish my child to be as smart as you are and as beautiful as I am," the actress explained.

"Well," the writer responded, "what if the child is as beautiful as I am and as smart as you are?"

Before my children were born I knew many theories of upbringing and had some pedagogical ideas of my own (of course, bright ones). In no way I am trying to compare myself with such great pedagogues as Pestalozzi or Dr. Spock, or somebody else of their stature, but I was sure that I knew a lot. After my children were born I realized that I knew nothing. Following my understanding I tried my best and put my whole soul, skills and knowledge into my children. Now I can see things about them of which I am proud, but it wasn't a theory—I followed my parent intuition.

Unfortunately, my approach appeared to have nothing to do with the theories I had. It was mostly my intuition, which apparently wasn't good enough and, thus, left plenty of room for criticism.

Indeed, when my son-in-law made some remarks and suggestions regarding my way of raising children, soon after marrying my daughter, I "swallowed" it silently remembering a joke. A teacher asked a young student, "Do you play a violin?"

"Have never tried but apparently I can," the student answered.

Long ago I passed the age when I was sure that "apparently I could play the violin."

To finish the parents' "sobbing" on an optimistic note I will tell a story about a professor who I knew since my college years. He had a late marriage and his son was born when he was already at a mature age. It was no wonder that he adored his only son. Once he came to a lecture-room proud and joyful. He interrupted his lecture and announced that his son, twelve, who for a long time considered his parents being foolish, admitted that the last two years they grew much wiser. When I recall the story I think with hope, "Thank God not everything is lost yet. Maybe someday I will grow wiser as well."

All these thoughts come now. The first thing that came into my mind then was where to live, how to support my children and provide a normal life for them. I had already done everything I could to solve our housing and other problems, and still our prospects didn't look too bright. More than once when somebody discussed family matters, I would return to these thoughts.

Meanwhile time passed. Dina was ten, Susanna was in her late thirties and further postponement increased the risk of possible pregnancy complications. All these considerations involuntarily lowered the requirements for the "right time." At some point Susanna began to speak more often with me on this matter. Regardless of what we were talking about, she frequently used to repeat, "I want a little boy, I want a little boy." She repeated it as a refrain. It became my wish as well and when Susanna found out that she was pregnant, we both felt happy.

Despite our concern Susanna's pregnancy was taking its normal course. Although my father-in-law was chronically ill and required a lot of care, when my mother-in-law learned about the event that she was waiting to occur for so long, she got excited. She was ready to begin caring for the baby immediately. Unfortunately, it never happened. She got gravely ill, and that was just the beginning of our troubles. An extremely difficult time came for us.

Susanna delivered the child two weeks later than she and her doctors had calculated. In her written message from the maternity hospital she wrote: "At 11 AM I delivered a boy, weight - 3600g, height - 53cm. Semochka (it is my diminutive name), I think I accomplished all your wishes: a boy, the day which was not 'unlucky' number 13 and no single extra day in the hospital. I have bolstered your shaken reputation (she meant that mostly girls were around me both at home and in my work team), so now you owe me." What she said about "not the 13," and the birth of the boy, is impossible to deny, but to present this and my "staggered reputation" as if it was my biggest concern were Susanna's additions in order to make me feel happier.

Before Vova's birth we didn't think a lot about the name for our future child. According to our tradition, parents of a newborn child wishing to memorialize some deceased close relative often choose a name after them. Both Susanna's parents and my mother were alive at that time. Dina was named after my deceased father. So, when after Vova's birth, my Uncle Yakov, who we loved very much, requested to name the newborn child after his brother Velvele who was killed in WWII we agreed to honor his request, naming the child Vladimir. Besides, by naming the child Vladimir we wanted to honor also our late friend and a wonderful person, Vladimir Aleksandrovich Dmitrievsky.

Many years have passed since then; the child became an adult and has his own children and every day fills us with great joy that we made the right decision during those hard times.

Twenty-Seven

In-Laws

1975 to 1976

My in-laws lived separately from us. They occupied the room where I lived with my mother during my bachelor years. Using public transportation, it took approximately twenty to thirty minutes to reach them from our home. My father-in-law had, as Russian doctors called it, a deep sclerosis. He was as helpless as a child. My mother-in-law took constant care of him even though, I guess, she needed help herself. She took care of them both, as long as she was able to walk and do something on her own.

When my mother-in-law's first stroke happened, every day after work Susanna went to her parents in order to take care of them while I was busy with our daughter Dina. After a while, Susanna's mother got better. That gave us some hope for her gradual recovery. Unfortunately, the hope appeared to be premature—the remission didn't last long.

The second stroke was much more severe than the first one. Later on, her neurologist told us about his serious suspicions that my mother-in-law's condition and some of her specific symptoms indicated a brain tumor. Was he right? We will never know. She was in a constant unconscious state and special care became necessary. It was just impossible to find any professional help, and if even we were able to find somebody to help, we couldn't afford it.

Our life turned into an everyday struggle. Most of the burden of the situation lay on Susanna's shoulders. When the second stroke happened Susanna was already several months pregnant. According to the Soviet laws, she could take a paid leave from work for two months before the day of the delivery that was predicted by her physician and two months after the actual delivery. During the last two months of her pregnancy, she took public transportation to commute to her parents' home every single day.

The actual leave before the delivery lasted two and a half months. Either her physician miscalculated or her pregnancy lasted two weeks longer. Every day of the last month of Susanna's pregnancy, we worried that she would give birth to the baby while on the street or in transit. She was commuting to her parents up to the day of the delivery. Fortunately, she gave birth in the hospital.

My mother-in-law's third stroke happened in the daytime, and their neighbor called us. Having no other options, we moved Susanna's parents to our place. They occupied one room, and we four lived in the second room. We both, but especially Susanna, were torn apart between her hopelessly ill parents, the newborn child, and Dina who all needed a great deal of attention.

Vova was a surprisingly quiet child. Sometimes it seemed that he understood what was going on. He never cried, even when being wet up to his ears. Nobody had an extra minute to check on him, devote some attention, or make sure that he didn't need anything. Of course, feeling enormous stress, Susanna stopped lactating after the first several weeks. Everything was like being in a haze: endless washing of swaddling clothes, changing them, taking care of the food for the child, feeding Dina, taking care of Susanna's helpless father and her dying mother, and many more daily problems... Nobody was able to help us.

My mother-in-law was dying in an unconscious state, and she remained unconsciousness up to her death. The last several days were especially difficult for Susanna. In vain, she was making incredible efforts to alleviate her suffering but nothing worked. She died in June, 1975.

The last several years of his life, Susanna's father was in a poor physical and mental condition though a silent and kind smile was as always on his face. After his wife's death, he didn't change a lot on the surface. He still could walk without anyone's help. Although he could eat by himself and perform the main vital functions, it was unclear if he fully understood what was going on around him. Even in his younger years, he wasn't an emotional or loud person. He was always considerate and delicate. I had never heard him complaining.

During the last years he was especially silent. He didn't talk, did what he was told to do without any comments, and didn't ask any questions. It was impossible to understand how he had perceived the death of his wife. For sure, he understood something and had an adequate reaction. I saw that along with his wife's death something died inside him. Being accustomed always to seeing his smile, I noticed, and that impressed me especially badly, that after his wife's death he completely stopped smiling.

I never saw him smiling again, regardless of what I did. I tried to communicate with him, to shake him up a little and somehow to improve his mood. It appeared to be just hopeless. He didn't smile and only a concentrated grave look gave away his emotions.

Although it was an ordinary January workday, Susanna and I were at home. Susanna took additional days off for taking care of nine-month-old Vova; I had a flexible workday and remained at home to help her. She was in the kitchen preparing food for Vova. My father-in-law and I were eating in the small room. I was watching him to make sure that he had everything necessary. The old man was in poor shape before but during the last several months he weakened even more. He had recently lost his dentures somewhere and wishing to help him eat, I cut all crusts from the bread leaving only the soft parts on the table.

We had almost finished eating when he began coughing slightly. He frequently coughed before, and a drink of water usually helped him. I gave him some water, but it didn't help. Then I gently patted his upper back, thinking that some crumbs got stuck in his throat. It didn't help either. He continued coughing more and more. It was becoming scary. I couldn't understand what was going on with him and called Susanna. She rushed into the room. The coughing became huskier and wasn't

119

stopping, although it didn't sound like he couldn't breathe. It seemed like something irritated his throat, and he continued coughing worse and worse. While I lifted him from the chair and bent him down to let the food get out, Susanna put her fingers in his mouth and pulled out some food remains. It still didn't help. No neighbors were around; there was nobody to call. I called the ambulance.

I can't say how long we waited for them, but when they came it was too late. They didn't tell us their diagnosis. Leaving us, the doctor suspected that the old man could have choked on bread or other food, or probably it could have been a stroke. During just a seven-month period Susanna lost both of her parents...

Twenty-Eight

The Blockade

1976

When I recall this experience, I have the feeling that even nature conspired against us and wished to add something unpleasant in our life. The previous ten months of that year the weather pattern didn't differ much from other years, and November seemed rainy as usual. But one night suddenly the air temperature fell below the freezing point and the entire city got covered with ice. Then snowfalls followed one after another. During the day the snow melted, and at night turned into ice. Odessa had little experience with such conditions because winters in Odessa were usually without snow and warm. To fight the ice, street sweepers covered the sidewalks with ash or salt to make them less slippery. However, the next day, under the southern Odessa sun, the ice and snow would melt, and after another night all the sidewalks were covered with slippery ice again. It still wasn't a major problem, until an occurrence that happened after a day or two that Odessians used to call the "blockade."

After the first snowfall and during the next several days the weather was unstable and the temperature fell below the freezing point many times. As a result, thick and heavy layers of ice covered electrical wires. The power lines didn't have any protection from ice, and the electrical wires were breaking, apparently, everywhere. It paralyzed transportation and other vital city services. The city sank into full darkness at night. Electrical pumps including water pumps didn't

121

work, and many main water lines were frozen or ruptured. In a few low-lying places, where some unfrozen water could have remained in the pipes, instead of water a gray-brown liquid ran with a lot of dirt and rust. The city was left without power, without water, without transportation. All of this was reminiscent of the conditions of the war blockade. It lasted a week or maybe even longer.

When the "blockade" happened, Vova was only seven months old, and the problems we experienced were quite nasty. Practically everything, including simple, elementary things transformed into problems, which for their solution required a lot of effort, creativeness, and even trickiness. Going somewhere became a problem: slippery sidewalks caused many broken bones and slippery roads caused many car accidents. For us adults, the shortage of food wasn't the worst problem, but we had nothing to feed Vova, and that was a problem. Every day we learned how to survive without many basic things, like water, power, transportation etc.

People really begin to understand the importance and value of water when they lack or don't have it at all. So the next "waterless" day, water management became our first priority. Equipped with a long pole I used to start my day by hunting for icicles. It wasn't an easy task because we lived in an area with three-story and taller buildings. Besides, we didn't need just any icicles; we needed only the absolutely clean and transparent ones. In our urban environment such a product was difficult to find.

Coming home with the "ice trophies," I selected the best icicles, then melted and boiled them—thankfully, the natural gas supply wasn't interrupted. Water purified in that way was the most precious product for us, because it was meant for little Vova to drink. The rest of the water we used carefully in tiny dosages for our needs. Wastewater, which was left from washing diapers, hands, dishes, etc. was utilized as well, and we collected it in a bucket for toilet-flushing purposes. One could see four buckets with dirty water lined up near our communal toilet. Thus, each single droplet of water was utilized, and at the same time people used to share drinkable liquids with each other.

I remember that a couple of days after the "blockade" had begun, my coworker had gotten three liters of milk for his child from somewhere.

He knew that I had a seven-month-old baby, and he shared it with me. At that time it was a real gift and helped us a lot.

Finally, when the weather improved and some time passed we got back to our routine life. Yet, for a long time when recalling the "blockade" days, the same thought kept coming to our minds: "What an easy life we have now." We had electricity; we had water; even lines for the toilet seemed less irritating. It was one more confirmation of the banal truth: "Everything is perceived by comparison."

Twenty-Nine

Fear and Fearlessness

1978 to 1987

While studying psychology, I came across an old book titled *Psychology of Fear and Fearlessness* (I am not sure of the exact title). The book was unrelated to my practical interest, and after browsing through it briefly, I put the book aside. But one phrase was etched in my mind because it was my thought as well: "There is no such thing as fearlessness, there is well-controlled fear." (It is my translation.) A part of the book was devoted to the ways of helping to overcome fear. Later I regretted my lack of curiosity but haven't been able to find the book again, even failing to remember whether it was an original book or translation.

I recalled the book because there were a couple of moments in my life which I wished I could have handled better. I still don't know the right answer. Those moments were engraved in my mind, and I would like to tell about them. All are situations which were connected with the fear of death.

It was a revelation for me that this feeling that everything is finite resides in many people regardless of their age. When we are young it doesn't come frequently to our mind that everything that had a beginning has to have an end. This truth related to people as well, and elderly people often think about it. As I recall, there weren't many old people around us. The only exception was our relative; we called him Uncle Yakov. He was the kindest person I ever knew and we all loved him. He was many years older than his wife, Aunt Eva, though nobody knew his exact age. His family, fearing "the evil eye," made a secret of his age. Uncle Yakov was well over eighty when his son got married. It was a long-desired marriage, and Uncle Yakov used to tell everybody that he dreamed to see his grandchildren. He did live to see his first and only grandson.

Many more years had passed since Uncle Yakov's grandson was born. I remember seeing the old man during one of my visits. He was depressed. I asked him, "What has happened, Uncle Yakov?"

He looked at me with tears in his eyes. "I want to live to see my grandson graduate from school."

I said sincerely, "Of course, you will." But then I didn't know what else to say.

A similar situation occurred when I visited my friend's father. The friend emigrated from the Soviet Union, but his father couldn't and remained in the country. He was close to eighty. It was one of my last visits before our emigration. I greeted him with the usual words, "How are you? How is your life?"

He bitterly replied, "What kind of a life is it if every day you expect to die?" I said something reassuring, but I wished I could say something better.

I was especially upset when once coming to our children's room I found Mom alone and crying. Mom was a courageous woman. I had never seen her crying without serious cause. I was frightened. "Mom, what happened?"

What she answered to me made my heart shrink. She said with sadness, "I don't want to die." I hugged and kissed Mom, and comforted her as I could. I clasped her gray head to my chest wishing to find the right words...

Those episodes are so deeply stamped in my mind. My father died in my arms; I witnessed Susanna's parents' death; I was old enough to understand many things; nevertheless, I didn't know and still don't know how to handle such situations.

Recently I recalled these episodes again. A dear friend of ours underwent surgery after which his doctor told him that he had at most six months left to live. Of course, his family and friends were devastated. He conducted himself courageously; I admired his spirit, though I saw how difficult it was for him. A question that crossed my mind in this connection was why the doctor told him that terrible news and his grave prognosis (which, fortunately, later appeared to be wrong).

I think that the close ones have to know the truth and prognoses but not the patient. What is the necessity or what are the merits of telling such things to patients? From my standpoint it is inhuman. Of course there could be exceptions but only exceptions. People if they are not criminals shouldn't live under the sword of Damocles. Life without hope isn't a life; it is just an existence, nothing else. And the doctor left our friend without any hope. His wife had recently died. It was a tragedy, but he handled the situation with unbelievable courage. I admired him; however, I couldn't bring myself to ask him how he managed to do it. I am afraid he was the only one who was able to answer that.

Thirty

Don't You Know What to Do?

1977 to 1980

When we moved to Lieutenant Lane, Dina was in the sixth grade. She was a capable girl, learned easily and had high grades in all subjects. In fact, she graduated from school with all the highest grades. She looked nice and attractive though a little older than her age. That sometimes caused funny situations. Once Dina, Vova and I were on a trolleybus, and I heard a passenger talking about me: "A guy with a young wife and a small kid."

The school she attended was an ordinary municipal school for children of both genders. Soon after World War II, all Soviet schools again became mixed schools where boys and girls were studying together. We heard from our friends and acquaintances that they had some typical teenage girl problems with their daughters. It especially related to clothes. Although during school hours students were required to wear school uniforms, after school girls liked to dress more casually. They could demand fancy dresses, which were frequently in short supply, costly, and not affordable for most parents. As for Dina, I have to say that she used to dress quite modestly. Probably she understood the matters of affordability and was satisfied with what she had. In any case, I don't remember Dina ever asking for anything expensive.

Another typical problem was dating and relationships between girls and boys. It wasn't something similar to what we see in America, like teenage pregnancy or drugs and violence. Most kids we saw behaved much more innocently, and the nature of problems was different. One common problem was that girls spent too many hours on dates, forgot about their classes and spent a lot of time at the dances staying out late in the evening.

I can't recall Dina dating anybody during her school years. Her relationships with boys in high school were unusual for a girl; she was fighting with them. She still had many rebukes in her school diary from her class teacher, but their nature changed from complaints about unstoppable chatting to complaints about her fighting with boys. However, the excuses were the same: it always was somebody else's fault; she was never guilty. Finally, she got the reputation of a combative girl for her way of solving problems with boys. When she complained to a teacher that a boy was harassing her, the teacher would tell her, "Don't you know what to do? Just punch him on the ear," and it wasn't clear if the teacher was being serious or just joking. To tell the truth, we didn't know how to react. Of course, we tried to restrain her, understanding that there was also a good side of that though: she would be able to stand up for herself. In time good changes came. As she was growing up, she was becoming less aggressive and more womanly and gentle.

More and more she was showing stronger leadership qualities. Apparently, there was a correlation between her relationship with boys and her leadership qualities which her teacher and I didn't notice; otherwise our reactions could have been more helpful.

In her senior classes, Dina showed an interest in painting. It is hard to tell if it was her own interest or that she got involved because of her friend Katya, who was attending painting classes. Anyway, I liked her enthusiasm. I bought her a portable easel with a tripod, and she tried to paint with watercolors. I also liked to draw, but to my great regret, in my school time in Odessa I had no opportunity to take art classes. So, I supported Dina's interest in art and in painting; regretfully, her involvement didn't grow into a serious passion. When she became a polytechnic institute student, she continued attending a painting group but gradually her interest in painting faded. Nevertheless, it was a nice experience; hopefully, some day it will occur again.

Dina's school offered practical classes for senior students. In those classes, students could choose to learn one of several specialties, including two of Dina's interests: decorative design and computational machines, which was the basics of mainframes. Students were supposed to get some practical knowledge sufficient enough to allow them to work immediately after graduation from school. When it became necessary to make a choice between the two practical classes Dina asked for my advice.

As far as I knew, the reality of making a living in decorative design as well as other kinds of art was too hard, even for a talented individual. (I suppose that it might not be exactly the same here in the U.S., but to some degree it is a similar situation). Understandably, I advised Dina to not miss the opportunity to choose the classes related to the computational technique, believing that if she would feel the craving for art she could always realize it. I didn't consider myself an expert but I was convinced that the computational industry had a promising and revolutionary future and witnessed how it was gaining strength. She followed my advice.

Now after having lived many years in America, I still would have given the same advice. I saw a good example when I learned about my classmate's daughter. Her mother was a music teacher; several members of their family had a musical gift, and even one of them was a distinguished musician. The daughter inherited the family musical talent. She graduated from a conservatory fortepiano class and then from the university with a major in computer science. She tried but couldn't make a living as a musician. However, music remained her strong passion. The only solution she found was to make a living as a computer engineer, and when she saved sufficient money periodically to devote herself to music. When her savings were gone she again began working in the computer science field for a while.

Looking back and thinking about Dina's decision, I may say that sometimes parents give useful advice, and Dina made the right choice.

Thirty-One

The "Pillow" Patient

1977 to 1980

When Dina was born my mother-in-law was alive, and she helped us to look after her. Dina began attending daycare when she was eighteen months old, and my mother-in-law continued helping us until Dina started attending school. We didn't have such luck with Vova. Soon after his birth, Susanna's parents died. At that time my mother was disabled. We had nobody to help us and were forced to put Vova into daycare when he was a little over twelve months old.

After we moved to Lieutenant Lane we were fortunate to find a kindergarten with daycare which was located just a couple of blocks away from our house. It was an ordinary but still fairly good daycare center. It was our luck that from an early age Vova was an agreeable, easygoing child, and we didn't expect any problems with this kindergarten. However, his first day, to our surprise he disliked something in his new place. He even cried a little when Susanna left him at the daycare. It was unusual for him, but we assumed that it was because of a new, unfamiliar place or new people, and we were sure that after a short while he would calm down.

In the morning of the next day, after leaving Vova at the daycare, Susanna went to work, Dina went to the school, and I was working at home. Somebody knocked on the door, and I went to see who it was. When I opened the door I was stunned: I saw Vova standing alone. He couldn't reach the doorbell and knocked on the door. I asked him what he was doing here, why he was alone, where his caretaker was, and so on. He was looking at me with big round eyes trying to explain something. Finally, I realized that he had just run away from the kindergarten.

Of course, I was upset with the kindergarten's care. What troubled me the most was that such a little child managed to escape from the daycare without anybody being aware. It wasn't funny to me at all. I asked Vova why he ran away. His answer killed me: he said that he didn't like the picture that was placed on his locker. They placed different pictures on the lockers instead of children's names in order to help them to find their lockers more easily. I also realized that when his caretakers would find out about his absence they would begin panicking. Nobody in our house had a telephone. As I was returning Vova to the kindergarten, we met his caretaker not far from our home. She was rushing to see us. The poor woman was white as a sheet and was so scared that she could barely speak. Although that "adventure" had a happy ending, for a long time after the incident we were extra vigilant. It was his first and, fortunately, last runaway.

Vova was growing up as a manageable and obliging child. It was enough to explain to him what we wanted, what was necessary to do and why, and he always did exactly what he was told. He was a man of his word.

As many kids, he showed a great interest in our routine chores, but unlike many kids of his age his interest was serious and steady. I still remember his big eyes, full of curiosity. He liked to watch how I was maintaining and repairing our car and appliances in the house. He could do it for hours, always ready to help. It gave me an opportunity to teach him how to use tools and work with his hands. I also took the opportunity to explain to him how things worked, some handyman's tricks and useful habits which I learned from others. He was a good listener, quickly absorbing my explanations and everything I showed him. When he became older he helped me in almost all repair works. He learned to do many different repairs, and now he has smart, skillful hands and does some things better than I.

When Dina was a child we had to spend a great deal of our time being with her when she went outdoors. It wasn't the case after we moved to Lieutenant Lane. We didn't have trouble letting Vova go outside the house; our backyard was a safe enough place for children's games. Everything would have been fine if we didn't have one serious problem that made us worry. His health was our constant concern and turned us into nervous wrecks. Usually the problem would start with a mild sore throat. We would do everything necessary to stop it. A couple of days later the sore throat would be gone and light coughing would begin. Then we would treat the coughing. Whatever we tried doing was useless. Despite our vigorous attempts at curing the coughing would progress and develop into bronchitis. And if not for the doctor's prescribing antibiotics, none of our efforts could stop the bronchitis from growing into pneumonia. It was so frustrating that we were on the verge of despair. Our doctor knew his condition and in such situations routinely prescribed antibiotics. The same doctor didn't get tired reminding us that the frequent usage of that medication was highly undesirable. Unfortunately, that wasn't the only problem with antibiotics.

At that time the Soviet pharmacological industry didn't produce antibiotic pills, and physicians used only antibiotic injections. Besides, the injections worked faster and more effectively. Depending on the conditions, they would prescribe one to four injections a day for up to ten days. There were no disposable syringes yet, and each injection procedure required substantial time. The most time-consuming part of the procedure was the sterilization of syringes and needles in boiling water prior to each injection. If the doctor prescribed antibiotics, nurses used to come to the patient's home and administer the injections.

When Vova had bronchitis, his doctors usually prescribed a dosage that required two injections. It wasn't always easy to get a nurse who could come twice a day, but somehow we managed to handle it. One time Vova's bronchitis was severe, and the doctor prescribed a dosage of antibiotics which required four daily injections. That became a problem for us. Our district policlinic couldn't provide a nurse who was able to attend four times a day. The policlinic nurse could schedule no more than one injection daily. We also couldn't find a private practice nurse who would be able to come even two times a day. The only alternative solution for the problem was to do the injections ourselves. Understandably that "ourselves" meant only "me": Since I had once "mumbled" something about becoming a medical doctor, now, when necessary to give injection I had no right to back down. And I didn't intend to.

I bought syringes, needles, a sterilization box, and tweezers. Then I spoke with my old friend Lilya, who always helped us by consulting and treating our children. She reminded me of some of the necessary basic rules I shouldn't forget and that I always had to be consistent before proceeding with the injections. The rules were simple and I remembered them as a priest remembers prayers. First: to sterilize everything in boiling water for at least twenty to thirty minutes prior to every injection and never touch the needles by hand. Second: to make sure that no air, not even a tiny bubble, got into the syringe. Air bubbles in blood are a deadly danger. Third: find the right spot at which to make the injection. Lilya taught me: "In your mind, divide a buttock by vertical and horizontal lines into four parts. Make the injection into the upper outer part. It is the least painful spot for an injection."

So theoretically Lilya gave me the fundamentals and armed with this vast knowledge I was ready to begin. However, to do it without experience and especially to your own child was a different story. My "tutor" advised me that I get some practice by making injections into a pillow. I followed her advice. The pillow had no complaints but couldn't replace a living being. I still didn't feel confident enough to do it to a small child with tiny buttocks and needed to practice on somebody more real than an insensible "pillow" patient. My body would be my first choice but my necessary body spots were beyond my reach.

I persuaded Susanna to be my real patient for the practice. She was ideal for the purpose; dealing with a real human being I would feel the full responsibility, have the necessary feedback, and gain more confidence that I wouldn't miss the right spot for the injection. I can't say that she was enthusiastic, but the situation was critical, and she sacrificed herself for a couple of aloe injections. Although she allowed me no more than two injections, it was a real training, and in any event, better than "forgiving" pillows. I did gain more confidence, and all the following injections on Vova became entirely my responsibility and I won his trust.

When Vova got bronchitis the first time, it wasn't a surprise because we understood that sometimes children did get ill. As Lilya said, for better health sometimes they had to be sick. But when the illness recurred again and again, with increasing frequency and with the same inevitable sequence, we became extremely worried. We consulted with all of the accessible doctors in Odessa. They told us that it could be an allergy or a problem with tonsils. To get one more opinion we decided to consult with Susanna's relatives, Fira and Lyova, whenever we had a chance. They were knowledgeable and reputable Kishinev pediatric (Fira) and pulmonary (Lyova) doctors.

It was late fall, when the four of us (actually, five: our dog Tvel, as always, was with us) rode to Kishinev in our car. Fira and Lyova thoroughly examined Vova and told us that according to their opinion his tonsils caused the problem. They recommended that his tonsils be removed, and they suggested it to be done in Kishinev under their care. Although the tonsillectomy was an inpatient procedure, it required some preliminary preparations. In any event, the summer was the best time recommended for the procedure, and we decided to wait until the end of spring.

Unfortunately our visit to Kishinev wasn't without adventures. When we arrived in the city I parked the car in Lyova's backyard, just under their bedroom windows. They lived in an apartment house that belonged to a junior technical college and was located on its land. We believed that it was the safest place we could pick. Susanna and I spent the night in Lyova's apartment, and next morning we found our car without the windshield. Somebody had stolen it. As we learned later that wasn't a unique incident: on the same night several more cars were "stripped." Not to mention the disgusting feeling I had seeing my car damaged and burglarized, I had a serious concern about our trip back home.

That day the weather was rainy and chilly. Vova had just recovered from another case of bronchitis. It was too risky to drive without a windshield, and we urgently needed to install a new one. For those who were unfamiliar with Soviet reality it might sound like a strange loss. The situation was really terrible for us. First of all, it was a weekend and all the shops were closed. Secondly, windshields were expensive and easy to remove and, thus, popular to steal. And third, all spare parts for cars, especially parts like windshields, were in short supply and were hard to find at any price. We were forced to postpone our return home. Lyova used all his numerous connections, and finally found people who installed a new windshield. Frustrated, tired, and under much stress, we finally went home.

The next summer Susanna and Vova returned to Kishinev where doctors were going to remove Vova's tonsils. The procedure was supposed to take place on a weekday, and I couldn't leave Odessa. I knew that a tonsillectomy wasn't a major surgical procedure, but I also knew that it could be painful and could have complications. Because of my worrisome nature I was nervous, especially on the day of the surgery. All that day, while I was driving my car, I constantly thought about Vova's procedure. These thoughts completely occupied my mind, distracting and preventing me from focusing on the road. As a result, when a car in front of me suddenly stopped, I was too late with the brakes. It was the one and only accident that was my fault for many years. In addition to my embarrassment, the driver whose car I "kissed" was a former colleague.

The surgery was successful, and at the end of the week Susanna and Vova were back home. We hoped that the tonsillectomy would stop Vova's endless bronchitis. Unfortunately, our hopes didn't come true. Although his cases of bronchitis became less frequent and weren't as severe, he still kept getting ill without any evident causes. Apparently, the tonsils were only a part of the problem.

The other part was allergies. We limited his consumption of certain, possibly allergic food and guarded him from other known allergens. From his early age he behaved as an adult and never violated the

135

restrictions. Well, maybe with one exception; just after we moved to Lieutenant Lane, he secretly ate a chocolate bar to which our neighbor had treated him. This "exception" cost him an extra case of bronchitis…

The year following the tonsil removal, Susanna took a vacation and went with him to the Crimean Peninsula where famous resorts specialized in breathing and lung problems for adults and children. Such types of medical centers were unique and the only ones in the country. It was difficult for ordinary people to receive treatment there but due to close to us people, my cousin, and his wife, who was a medical doctor and lived in the Crimean city of Eupatoria, it appeared to be possible for us. The first day Susanna and Vova arrived in Eupatoria, Vova got ill. Susanna was in despair. Benedict and Anya helped them get the treatment. Vova took a full course of the special treatment, but again it didn't help a lot. The problem was solved later after I returned from Moscow where I had been attending extension courses at the Moscow Institute of Energy. How I did it I'll tell you in the next chapter.

Thirty-Two

Anthem to Jogging

The significance of an event in our personal life frequently depends not only on its scale, but it also depends on the magnitude of its impact on our life. A small jump isn't a big deal. Small jumps repeated regularly every day for many years could be a big deal. Regularity can make a difference because it becomes a habit. Someone said, "Sow action—shall reap habit, sow habit—shall reap character, sow character—shall reap fate." One such "small jump" for me was the beginning of jogging.

Except for a not so smart habit of smoking, which I developed in my college years and quit years later with great difficulty, I always tried to follow a reasonably healthy lifestyle. I used to start every morning with physical exercise, and whenever I had the time and the opportunity I liked swimming, or walking and hiking, or exercising with dumbbells, or I did other sporting activities. Although I did exercise as often as possible, it wasn't a regular part of my daily routine. I felt that I needed something more, and I did have good intentions, but I couldn't decide what to do specifically. One occasion helped me.

When I was in Leningrad on a business trip, I saw a thin book on my brother Roma's bookshelf. I remember that the book was a Russian translation from English and was written by an Australian or New Zealand author. The title of the book, and this is as close to a translation that I can attempt from the original Russian, was *Running for the Sake of Life.* The author of the book described his experience of regular running or jogging and what a great impact it had on his health and shape. I read the book and found that the author's experience and medical references were pretty convincing and exciting. I considered trying it myself.

On returning home, I made up my mind to start running daily after work and before dinner. I followed all of the author's recommendations regarding dress, shoes, gradual loading, etc, and I managed to jog for two weeks without breaking my routine. Then I needed to stop for two days to see to some business matters, then some days I felt tired, then something else came up and, before I knew it, I hadn't been running for over two weeks.

The second attempt ended in the same manner, and I started to question my daily schedule because there was definitely something wrong with it. Every day I had some new excuses not to run. After rethinking my schedule again and again, I came to the conclusion that the best time for running would be in the morning, before work and before breakfast.

I began a third attempt to make jogging a regular activity, and that attempt was a success because I was determined to do it every morning. For the next thirty years I jogged for between thirty and sixty minutes every morning. I jogged when I was on business trips, even when ill, and I continued it all through my six-month stay in Italy and my eventual immigration to the USA.

Now, having had such a long jogging experience, I can say that, though jogging can't be and isn't a panacea for curing or preventing all illnesses, nevertheless, jogging is definitely a great benefit for our health and shape. I am speaking about my personal experience. Jogging helped me a lot by keeping me in good physical shape and often in good mental shape as well. I strongly believe that jogging helped me to overcome many stressful situations.

While jogging, I learned how to do many things, not the least of which was never to waste time. At the beginning, during jogging, I would think about different problems and events, like my personal, social and work problems, which occupied my mind. I tried, and many times was successful at solving some technical, scientific, and engineering problems while I was jogging.

I even managed to study English while running because after we submitted our applications to emigrate my jogging time was the only time when I could gain and improve my English vocabulary. I prepared special flash cards with English words on one side and the corresponding Russian translations on the other side, and then during the jogging I tried to memorize them playing a game with myself. As soon as I arrived in America I used my time jogging—later, walking— to listen to news and other broadcast programs, and it was one way in which I significantly improved my spoken English.

Jogging served me well. And I would say not only me, but I am glad to mention that due to my belief in jogging many of my acquaintances began jogging as well. I encouraged and "infected" them with this healthy habit. Most of all I am happy that jogging helped my son Vova get rid of his endless attacks of bronchitis.

During my four-month stay in Moscow, in 1984, communication with my family wasn't as frequent as I would have liked: home telephone installation still remained an unsolvable problem. The only way we were able to exchange information was through mail. Knowing my restless, easily agitated character, Susanna didn't want to upset me and kept silent regarding Vova's condition. To all my questions about Vova's health, Susanna kept writing to me that everything was okay. When at the end of December I returned to Odessa, I learned that during my absence Vova had bronchitis and not only once. The news was troubling and my reaction was immediate and resolute: "Enough is enough, something radical has to be done, otherwise it will never stop." I told Susanna, "Starting from tomorrow he will begin jogging with me."

My decisiveness wasn't groundless. Although at that time jogging wasn't as popular as nowadays, I had witnessed good examples of its benefits. First of all, my own long personal experience in jogging showed a definite positive effect, though being relatively young I didn't feel any considerable problems in my physical condition, but I wanted to maintain good physical shape and jogging helped me to do that.

The second example was impressive. I started my jogging "career" when we lived on Sverdlova Street. The closest suitable place to my home for running was a big town square, called "Kulikovoe Pole," where many people used to walk and rest with their children and pets. Sometimes while jogging in the morning I saw a man who was often sitting on the park bench. He had a gray face, unusual for an Odessian, and appeared to be in his late forties or early fifties. He drew my attention because of his long, hoarse coughing that made me think that he was a heavy smoker. I had never seen him smoking though. He followed me with a long look but had never tried to talk to me.

Later, after we moved to Lieutenant Lane, I chose for my running route one of the coastal park paths. The park area was deserted, and it was a rare occasion to meet anybody. One day I bumped into a jogger, who appeared to be the "coughing man." It amused me how his appearance had changed. His cheeks weren't ash-gray anymore—they had a normal, even slightly pinkish color. Seeing me, he stopped and I stopped as well. This time he wasn't afraid to talk. He asked why I had disappeared from the Kulikovoe Pole; he was looking for me, wishing to ask some questions. I laughed and asked why. He briefly told me his story. I don't remember the details, but he had inhaled some chemical vapors and had gotten himself into a serious lung problem. A heavy cough was literally choking him and doctors failed to help.

He had read something about the health benefits of running but wasn't sure about it and most importantly felt too shy about running. I was the first person he saw running in a public place and my example had inspired him to make up his mind. When we met he had already been running for several years, and his cough had almost disappeared or at least had become much lighter and less frequent.

I explained to Vova why I wanted him jogging with me. There was not a word of objection from him. The word came from Susanna. She was worried if winter was the right time to start. Indeed, that year the winter in Odessa was extremely cold, and the temperature stayed below zero Celsius (and sometimes considerably lower) for a long time. Several times unusually deep snow fell and didn't melt. We lived close to the sea, and windy weather in the wintertime was frequent.

That year we even experienced many blizzards with bone-chilling winds. Maybe it wasn't really the best time to start, but I didn't want any postponements.

So, Vova began running with me. He wasn't scared by the weather and was running with willingness. He liked the challenge. The entire winter Susanna had arguments with me about how Vova should be dressed for running. As a typical mother, she had endless worries that he wasn't dressed adequately for the cold weather and being underdressed and sweating he could get a cold. There were many other worries. In vain I tried to explain that from my experience excessive clothing could make sweating worse. It was only after a while, seeing that nothing bad happened, that she trusted me more and gradually calmed down.

The winter passed, then spring passed, and with no single occasion of bronchitis or colds, or even a runny nose. Step by step I was increasing the distance and time of Vova's running. The jogging became part of his morning routine. After that, we jogged together in Odessa, then in Austria and Italy during the six months of emigration, and then in America. He continued jogging as long as he lived with us until he entered the University of California at Berkeley. After moving to the campus, he stopped running as regularly as he used to but other kinds of active sports became a part of his lifestyle.

There could be discussions about the usefulness of jogging, nevertheless the fact remained that as long as he continued his morning runs, his problems with bronchitis, colds, etc. never occurred again. They were completely gone.

Thirty-Three

Belated Regrets

1976 to 1983

After we moved to Lieutenant Lane, my mother used to come every year to live with us in Odessa for seven to eight months. Usually it was at the warm time of the year from the middle of spring to the end of fall. At the beginning, she shared a room with the children. It was inconvenient for the children and difficult for her. The only small advantage in that situation was that she had an opportunity to be with the children, whom she loved very much. However, things changed after her second surgery. Her speech was impaired and the children had difficulty understanding her and that appeared to be a painful experience for her. She couldn't handle her frustration and preferred not to speak unless it was an urgent necessity. She did have pleasure just watching them.

With years, her health worsened and she needed more attention. We worked and the children were at school or institute. In the morning we used to leave her food, medicine, and everything necessary with detailed instructions on what and when to take it. When we came home in the evening, we saw that she had forgotten to take either the medicine or the food. Sometimes she didn't even touch what was left for her. Things became worse when, periodically, she began experiencing some new problems; sometimes she behaved strange, hallucinated, or tried to go somewhere. Doctors attributed it to her sclerosis, but I was not so sure. Most likely it was a side effect of her medications.

Once, when I was on my way home, suddenly I saw Mother on the street half-dressed, lost, confused and going nowhere. I asked her what was going on and where she was going. She couldn't answer. I took her home, and after a while she seemed to get better. We had never locked the door when leaving her without keys, hoping that the neighbors would help her if she asked for it. However, after that incident, fearing that she could do it again, I fixed a hook outside of the entrance door. When we all had to go out and leave her alone, we kept the hook locked to be sure that Mother wouldn't get out. Now I understand it was dangerous decision. Luckily, my work was located a five- to ten-minute walk from our house, and I was able to drop by two or three times during my working hours. I could see what Mother was doing and take care of her. Still it is hard for me to comprehend how she managed to do anything without help and not hurt herself while nobody was at home.

In the normal meaning of these words, there weren't nursing homes in Odessa, and I think in the entire Soviet Union. The conditions in homes for lonely elders who had nobody to take care of them were miserable beyond imagination. As bad as they were it was still impossible to be admitted. Anyway, even if the care were better, we would never have peace of mind and have considered that as an option. We wanted Mother to be with us.

Life with the children in the same room created for Mother some feeling of closeness and communication with them. But when she was tired and needed a rest, she had no place to go. Neither Mom nor the children had privacy. Although the cramped conditions weren't a problem for Vova because of his age, for Dina, already a teenager, it was a serious problem. Regardless of how hard we tried to make things better, we couldn't find an acceptable solution. Needless to say, it was difficult for all of us and especially for Mother.

Later on, hoping to ease the situation, I put a small folding bed (camp cot) in my "study" where Mother could sleep. It didn't help much because the study was so tiny (less than fifty square feet) that Mother couldn't go to bed or get up without our help. She needed a place where she could sleep, rest, watch TV, have a nap or just to stay alone for a while, and the bathroom-sized "study" wasn't a solution. Mom desperately needed some privacy.

The only solution was to exchange her Leningrad room for one in Odessa. Apartment exchange was a long and painful process taking several lengthy stages to get to what one wanted, and each step was a big event. Besides, the exchange couldn't happen soon.

Also, Mother's trips from Leningrad to Odessa and back were becoming extremely difficult for her. She was afraid to fly and preferred traveling by train. A trip between Leningrad and Odessa usually took thirty-six hours by rapid train. Railway transportation had all kinds of sleeping cars, and Roma used to drive Mother to the train and put her into her compartment. Then upon her arrival in Odessa, we met her and I drove her home. Passengers from Mother's compartment usually helped her during the trip. But each year Mother's health got worse; her trips became a terrible ordeal for her. She could hardly travel, especially alone.

After one of her trips she came to Odessa in such a poor condition that we couldn't let her go back alone. Susanna took several days off and went with her to Leningrad. We understood that the trips had become a true torture for Mother, and she shouldn't and wouldn't travel alone anymore. Until we were able to find an acceptable solution, Mom continued to live with my brother in Leningrad; he took care of her. I saw her periodically, mostly when I had business trips to Leningrad.

It was on a warm March morning that I was speaking with our neighbors in the backyard when a mailman brought a telegram. The telegram was from my brother, Roma. The words were simple: "Mother died." I read the telegram again and again and refused to believe what I read. The meaning of the words just didn't reach my mind. Mom's living face was before my eyes. I called Susanna, and then went to the institute. That day, in the afternoon, I had a lecture at the institute. My students crowded near the door ready to leave the auditorium, however, after seeing me, they returned to the class. Incidentally, at that time the institute administration, in its bureaucratic zeal, evaluated professors' competence by the number of minutes they were late for classes (It is hard to believe but it was an order from the institute authorities). How I managed to lecture I don't remember; I spoke like a robot, barely realizing what I was speaking about.

The next day I flew to Leningrad. Roma told me that Mother died in her sleep or seemed to be sleeping when she passed away. After an examination by the ambulance doctor, she was taken to the morgue.

When I arrived in Leningrad, we went to the morgue in order to make an arrangement for the burial. The morgue employee told us that before the burial arrangement we should confirm Mother's body.

It was the typical Soviet service. Nobody had bothered to prepare the body for the confirmation. They hadn't even covered the body with some kind of cover or sheet. I was devastated seeing the dearest person to me in such a condition. The scene before my eyes was so cruel and inhuman that even after many years have passed, I still recall that picture with anger and bitterness; when I remember it I am shaken from pain and rage. Mom was lying in a position of a person fallen from a roof. I saw her naked body, her gray hair and felt a sharp pain in my chest. Even now, I have not the strength to describe all the details. One wouldn't say that the morgue employee did it intentionally. I believe that he sympathized with us but didn't understand what he was doing. In no civilized society could such a thing happen. Over sixty years of the communist ruling had dehumanized the people and eliminated their capacity to act with feeling.

Mom's body was cremated. Later, I took the urn with the ashes to Odessa. When Roma visited us, we brought the urn to Father's grave and buried it next to his tombstone. I remember how hard I took my father's death. I was much younger, and the mortality of my parents had never come to my mind. My father's death was my first big loss. My mother outlived him by more than twenty-five years. When she died I was forty-seven, a family man with two children. I already knew something about life and death; many of our close relatives were gone. I understood that there was no immortality in this world; all of us are mortal. But when Mother died I had a feeling that I became more than an orphan; I lost not only the dearest, utterly devoted, loving person, but I lost a part of myself.

After Father's death and for the rest of her life Mother was ill. Without Father we had a hard time. It was especially difficult for Mom. Suddenly, she became alone, without her dearest man, without the support she had, and with illnesses which pursued her one after another. They seemed to all come together, and she desperately struggled with depression.

However, life went on and many things required my attention. My mind was occupied by thoughts about the future, about my work and my life, and then, later, about my own family, and other vital things. And despite all that, despite numerous difficulties in our life, all the following years I had done my best to make her life easier, more comfortable, to treat her diseases, to help her. It seemed I did what I could.

Nevertheless, after Mother's death more and more frequently my mind returned to previous years when Mother was alive. The same thought throbs in my head that what I did for her wasn't enough, that I should have done more even though we lived in different cities. I keep asking myself questions. Had I been energetic and insistent enough in solving her housing problem, her move to Odessa? Maybe I should have been more actively involved in her life. There can be many "maybes."

When she lived in Odessa I tried to guard her from all our numerous problems and difficulties. By no means was my silence a lack of understanding or sympathy for her. It was rather a lack of sharing with her our everyday events and concerns. Something certainly was missing. A close, dear and especially an ill person shouldn't be left on her own. Usually we believed that by not telling Mother our routine troubles we were protecting her. Now we understand that it was wrong. Sharing with her at least some of the family matters could bring her a sense of participation, togetherness, and make her life more fulfilled. Many things I understood later, too late. Belated regrets. The realization that nothing can be changed, that it is impossible to turn time back, makes my feeling of guilt even deeper.

My mother with Dina

Thirty-Four

The First Car Trips

1976 to 1987

I bought a car in 1976, and soon was ready for trips. Before starting my first long voyage, I had to think about many things which could occur during the trip, and among them, the children were my primary concern. Dina was thirteen and old enough not only to take care of herself but also to help us. On the other hand, she was still a child and needed a lot of attention. Vova was a little over two years old and had some allergy problems, which weren't extremely severe at that time; nevertheless, he required a lot of attention.

We also had one more member of our family with us who wasn't easy to handle. I am talking about "His Doggy Majesty," Tvel, who, beyond the general care, needed a special eye kept on him because he could get into predictable and more frequently unpredictable trouble. We were forced to take him with us. He didn't obey anybody except me (and sometimes Susanna), and nobody could take the responsibility of looking after him for so long. There wasn't such a thing as an all-day dog care service in Odessa nor do I believe in the whole country. Besides, we wouldn't have felt comfortable leaving him with strangers.

Taking into consideration that Vova was still young (actually, a little baby) and it was my first long trip, I wanted to minimize the distance we drove each day to six to eight hours. Secondly, for the same reasons, I preferred to spend the night with people I knew and we could stay with two to three days and spend some time to enjoy talking with relatives and friends.

My plan included cities: Kherson, Dnepropetrovsk, Poltava, Tula (near Moscow), and Kiev. In each of these cities we had somebody we wanted to see. There was also Kursk and a couple of other places along our way where we knew no one. The trip was supposed to take about three weeks if nothing unpredictable happened. I tried to foresee everything I could think of, realizing that in our circumstances everything, literally everything, even small things could be a problem. My equipment list included a tent, sleeping bags, blankets, tools, some dry and canned food, a medicine chest, spare clothes, and many other necessary (and maybe not necessary) things. Suspecting that gas stations could be sparse or be out of gas, I even put a spare twenty-liter gas can into the trunk. As it proved later, my suspicions were true on several occasions, and the spare can of gas was helpful. After all the preparations our car resembled a moving house or rather a fortress on four wheels.

When the day to leave arrived, the team members took their places in the car according to the "staff schedule," and we started our journey. Susanna was sitting next to me; the kids plus full-of-worry Tvel occupied the back seat. At the beginning, everybody was so excited and enjoying the sense of driving and looking around; nobody wanted to miss a thing. All "teammates" were rolling their heads, exchanging comments, and asking questions. Then, after a while, the road became more monotonous, curiosity was satisfied and questions were exhausted.

We didn't have any connections with the outside world: the car wasn't equipped with a radio. Having no food for conversation or points of discussion, the initial activity gradually faded away. Dina unsuccessfully tried to read. The ride was rocking her to sleep, and gradually all of the back-seat passengers fell asleep. Dina was resting on the back seat; Vova was resting on top of her, and calmed-down Tvel was sleeping on top of Vova like a cat under the sun stretching his legs toward the front seats. All three had a good time and wonderful dreams. Susanna was struggling to stay awake. She vigilantly watched me too, talking to me, asking something, and trying to keep me alert. Sometimes, she lost the battle and fell asleep though not for long.

It didn't bother me to see her dozing off. I enjoyed driving, though not always and not everything was enjoyable. I felt extremely strained. The thought that all my family was in the car and I had no right for a mishap didn't leave me for a second. I felt a huge responsibility for their safety, their lives and well-being. It wasn't just the concern of a person with a great imagination. There were no freeways in the USSR. Soviet interstate roads were similar to poor highways by American standards or even compared to many European countries. There were a few roads with two lanes in each direction, but most roads were two-lane roads with just one lane in each direction. Not a single road had a solid dividing wall or a median strip. Most roads, especially the main ones, were heavily overcrowded.

Many trucks were moving wearily slowly. It was just impossible to follow them for hours, and when drivers saw any opportunity, they tried to pass the slower-moving vehicles. Passing was the most dangerous maneuver due to oncoming traffic. The tiniest mistake or miscalculation could cost a life… In addition to that problem many roads were in a poor state. Driving in such conditions required constant alertness and full attention. Any distraction could be fatal. No responsible driver could afford even the slightest relaxation.

The next problem we experienced was where to spend the night, especially if something happened in the middle of nowhere. I minimized the number of places we stayed where we didn't have relatives or acquaintances. Nevertheless, long distances between some cities and road conditions sometimes forced us to stop for a night in unplanned and unfamiliar places. Our problems will be more understandable if I tell the reader that there was a severe shortage of hotels practically everywhere and with time the situation hadn't improved a lot. Even the word "motel" didn't exist in our lexicon.

It took a lot of luck to find a place to stay overnight. Only once on that trip we were lucky to find a vacant place in a tiny hotel, and it was available only for Susanna with the kids. I slept in the car. At other times, when we weren't so lucky, we made stops near public buildings or somewhere close to an accessible toilet. Susanna with the children and Tvel slept in the car, which I parked on the street or wherever it was possible. As for me, I would spend the night next to the car in the sleeping bag. I wouldn't say it was convenient; but when you are young many things are more acceptable.

My driving experience began with trips to Moldavia, the tiny neighboring republic that wasn't larger than the Odessa region. Susanna's relatives, better goods and food supply, and proximity to Odessa were the main reasons which made Moldavia so attractive for our short trips. The Moldavian roads were my first road "training grounds."

Roads, roads… It is hard to describe how poor and dangerous they were in most parts of the USSR. To be constantly alert became my rule, and if I happened to break it, a punishment was inevitable.

We were in Moldavia heading back to Odessa after a short trip. As usual, the whole family was in the car. It had rained all night and periodically during the day, not too heavy though, and it seemed there was nothing to worry about. So I didn't pay much attention to many small and larger puddles along and on the road. Sometimes several dozen yards of the road were covered with water; luckily, the pools weren't too deep and didn't obstruct the drive.

Therefore, when I drove into the next large puddle, it didn't worry me much; continuing to drive I just slowed down. After a while I noticed that the car was moving into deep water. I stopped the car and looked around. We found ourselves in the middle of a lake. It wasn't difficult to understand that somehow I lost the road and missed the point when it was still possible to back down or turn around safely. I decided to go slowly forward, hoping that we had already reached the deepest point.

My prognosis appeared to be wrong. After a couple of dozen yards, suddenly, the car started to skid. I looked out from the window and saw that the water was high; so high that it was impossible to open the doors. What worried me tremendously was that if we got into deeper water it could kill the engine. We were trapped, and as bad luck would have it, not a living soul was around. Susanna got nervous. "I told you to be careful," she said and as always she was right, but at that time it was a little too late. Nothing threatened our lives; however, the situation was unpleasant.

It took some time for me to calm down a little and begin attempts to get out from the trap by carefully moving the car back and forth. Intuitively I felt that the right wheel was skidding more than the left one. I asked the kids to move to the left side of the car and take Tvel with them—at least he was an additional couple of pounds of useful weight. The move was right and the car stopped sliding. I made one more, as it appeared, good decision: I drove forward. Soon, we were again on the right road and gradually found the way out of the "lake." Later I visited this place again and seeing many huge and deep pits understood that the situation wasn't unpleasant—it was quite dangerous.

A similar situation, though less dramatic, took place again in Moldavia. It is necessary to mention that Soviet roadmaps weren't updated frequently enough and weren't reliable either—apparently, to confuse enemies and spies. Many times, after studying roadmaps we still weren't sure about directions and were forced to ask other drivers which way was better to go or which road was better to take.

We were going to the Moldavian capital, Kishinev. After driving for over an hour, we saw a new road which wasn't shown on the map. I stopped and began asking approaching drivers where the road led. One driver explained to us that it was a new road to Kishinev, exactly where we were going to, and encouraged us to take it.

This new road looked so nice and so tempting we took it asking no more questions and headed for the city. Soviet drivers weren't spoiled by good roads, and the road was really good—without cross-sections, relatively wide, compared to many other roads, smooth, and built from concrete slabs with tightly closed junctions. Our way was mostly through a forest which made the drive especially pleasurable. "One has to pay for the pleasure," I recalled this saying, when after a couple of hours of driving, the road abruptly ended in the middle of nowhere with a step, two or three feet high. Luckily, I stopped in time; there wasn't a way ahead. Only then it came to my mind that we saw no other cars on the road. Strangely enough, it didn't alert me before, probably because of a similar situation when I drove from Kursk to Tula and for hundreds of miles we met only a few cars.

Nevertheless, the story had an almost happy ending. After looking around I noticed a dirt road not far away from us. It was logical to assume that the dirt road was used to bring the road slabs, and it had to go to Kishinev. My initial enthusiasm quickly faded when it appeared that the difference in levels between slabs of the pavement and the dirt road was two feet. There was no way that we could jump down off the road. I turned back and luckily before long found a more or less safe descent to the temporary road. Finally, after many zigzags we found the way out.

Not all of our trips had happy endings. One of them was quite frustrating. It started as usual, even better than usual. Not long before the trip I became the happy owner of four brand-new Prostor tires. ("Prostor" is a brand). The explanation for my happiness was simple. My car had such poor "shoes" that a thirty-mile trip could have been risky. For two or three years I looked for new tires, and my friend—in exchange for a big favor that he did for somebody else—managed to buy four new tires for me. One of my old tires served as a spare tire. To call it a "spare tire" was an exaggeration. With great caution I could drive on it no more than a few miles. But the possession of four new tires inspired my confidence that I would never need a replacement. It is well said: "Never say never."

Equipped with new "shoes" we went on a long trip to the Northern European part of the Soviet Union. The city of Kiev was supposed to be our first stop. To my surprise, the road wasn't too overcrowded and I drove at the maximum allowable speed. Several hundred kilometers was already behind us when I felt that the car began veering to the right side of the road. While I was thinking about what could be happening, I felt that it was becoming harder to hold the steering wheel in my hands. This sign was alarming, and I began to brake slowly and did it just in time. At the end of the braking several loud popping sounds were heard from the right side under the car.

When I stopped and examined the wheels I saw that the front right tire had blown out. Miraculously, we avoided a major accident. I checked the wheel to find the cause of the tire failure. There were no nails in the tire and the valve worked fine. At the side of the tire one could see a big bulge. A closer look showed that because of a manufacturing defect several reinforcing tire cords were broken and resulted in irreparable damage. It wasn't hard to guess that the broken cords caused the loud popping sounds. My mood deteriorated completely. I thought with irony and great sadness that one of the new tires, which were so difficult to obtain, was totally lost. I installed the spare wheel but still couldn't continue the trip. The spare wheel actually wasn't a spare; it was as bald and fragile as a worn-out shoe. In addition to all that, the brand and diameter of the spare wheel didn't match the other tires. We urgently needed a tire of the same brand.

The silver lining in that was that the accident happened just a few kilometers from the city of Belaya Tzerkov (White Church). By a happy coincidence, the plant where my tires were manufactured was located in this city. It gave me some hope. I assumed that presenting them with the defective tire I at least would be able to buy a new one. We had no options left, and I made my way toward Belaya Tzerkov. When we arrived at the tire plant the picture we found shocked me.

Next to the plant, we saw a big improvised car camp which was similar to a motorized Gypsy encampment. There were all kind of cars and trucks. Tents could be seen near some cars. There were a few families but most drivers were alone, and all the campers were looking for tires. What I learned then made me feel that the worst of my premonitions appeared not to forebode the worst to come.

From time to time mysterious individuals appeared in the camp, mainly in the dark, and the lusting crowd rushed toward them. The mysterious guys were local speculators; although they looked like ordinary drivers, people recognized them with a "sixth sense." The luckiest had a chance to whisper with them for a few minutes, and then the "distinguished contracting parties" disappeared. It meant that the speculator and drivers struck a bargain regarding the tires' price and delivery, and the guys went to get the "goods."

During the daytime some drivers managed to find plant workers and make a deal with them. The plant workers knew a couple of secret places in the plant fence where after making a deal they could throw the tires over the fence. For all the time we were in the camp, we hadn't seen any militiamen (Soviet policemen), but undoubtedly the city authorities knew about the camp activity well. Militiamen knew exactly how much they would be paid to keep their eyes closed and when to open them.

We came to the camp in the afternoon and the rest of that day I spent gathering information and familiarizing myself with the general situation. The next day I went to the plant. A plant clerk told me, "I don't see any defects in the tire. In order to get a replacement you have to prove that the tire had a defect."

"A bad cord is a hidden defect but you can clearly see a bulge. It is the proof. What else could be more convincing, what else do you want me to present to you?" I asked.

"It is your business," the clerk passed back. Any further discussion was useless. I asked if there was a chance to buy a new tire, otherwise we couldn't drive home. The clerk was like a stone wall: "It isn't my problem; the plant isn't a store."

Dina didn't like the idea of spending one more sleepless night in the camp. To tell the truth, we were all tired from the bedlam; besides, chances of getting a tire were slim. I also didn't feel it was great fun dealing with the jackals like second-hand dealers or getting a tire over the fence. On the other hand, it was too risky to have a poor tire and without a spare to continue the journey. So we were forced to interrupt the trip and, as fast as our spare wheel allowed us, drove home.

Despite this discouraging experience we didn't give up the idea of taking a trip that summer. As we learned, my cousin's family was planning a short, seven- to eight-day car trip. They invited us to join them, and with the given timeframe and mutual interest, the West

SOL TETELBAUM

Ukraine and Moldavia seemed like the best route. I had borrowed a couple of used tires that were still in drivable conditions, and at the end of the summer, we hit the road. Boris was with his wife Lora and drove their car. I was with Susanna and Vova. After the wonderful experience we had recently, Dina preferred to remain at home and spend the rest of the summer vacation with her friends. She wanted us to take Tvel; though, I think he wasn't excited about going anywhere.

We were traveling through Moldavian meadows and West Ukrainian forests, which after Odessa's monotonous and flat steppe landscape pleased our eyes. Only Tvel didn't enjoy the traveling. The poor old guy preferred to stay at home. He cried and fiercely scratched himself. We attributed it to his chronic vitamin deficiency (beriberi); nevertheless, troubled with his constant crying I checked him to see what was going on. We found a myriad of fleas on him. It was simply unbelievable. Just before the trip we had thoroughly washed and combed him. But, having a previous bad experience with flea remedies, we were afraid to use any chemicals. How and where he managed to invite those crowds of predators was hard to imagine. The only thing I can say is that the poor animal suffered a lot.

We were forced to change our route and look for a lake or some other body of water. Luckily, a small river wasn't far from us. We washed Tvel many times and kept him in water as long as possible hoping to drown all those hordes of bloodsuckers. Our success wasn't great, though he got some relief, at least for a while. Unfortunately, fights with Tvel's fleas became routine and probably I would have forgotten this episode on the next day, but what made me remember it was the almost human gratefulness I read in the dog's eyes after we washed him.

The brave team in Kishinev
(From left to right)
Solomon, Susanna's aunt, Vova, Dina, Susanna, Tvel

Thirty-Five

Road Adventures

1977 to 1985

All of our car trips had a great deal of exciting and sometimes dramatic moments and I am going to tell about some such trips.

We were traveling in the North Caucasus. According to our schedule the goal for that day was to reach a place that was located near one of the main Caucasus routes. Wishing to make our way shorter, I decided to take a small route, which connected two key roads and was shown on the map as a regular road.

When I turned onto that route we found that it was a narrow dirt road with many zigzags and a few wider strips where two cars from the opposite directions were able to pass by each other. Almost all the way down the road, vertical rocks limited its left side, and the right side of the road was on the verge of a deep gorge. None of that seemed encouraging. I believed that such conditions would be only at the beginning, and then, after a short drive, it would become a regular two-way road with asphalt pavement. My assumption appeared to be dead wrong, and I realized it too late: I had already driven quite a long distance. Besides, there wasn't a place where it would be possible to turn around and drive back. The road was going up and up and I continued to drive with the speed of a snail, cursing myself for my naïve trust in the map. All my passengers, including Tvel blissfully happy on top of the children, were sleeping like newborn babies during a monotonous drive and hot sun.

At some moment I felt that I had to check the brakes, because when I was braking on a rise it seemed that the car was slightly moving back. I stopped the car and got out to check them. When I checked the left wheels, its brakes and tires had nothing suspicious. But when I tried to look at the right side of the car, I got a sinking sensation in the pit of my stomach. I saw that the right side of the road didn't have a shoulder and the roadway ended with a steep and deep slope. The most horrifying sight was that the ground under the rear right wheel sank, and a big piece of it broke off and fell down. The wheel hung over the gorge.

My first instinct was immediately to awaken Susanna and children and get them out of the car as soon as possible. Then a scary thought suddenly burned my mind: any incautious stirring, the slightest disturbance of the car's equilibrium, and the car would lose its stability and slide down in the gorge. It could be a disaster. This thought made me chilly.

With great effort I kept myself from panicking. Everything inside me was shivering. It is hard to say for how long I was thinking—I saw the only way out. Picking up a couple of stones I shoved them behind the front and rear left wheels to prevent the car from moving back. Then extremely carefully, I got into the car, started it and began slowly inching forward. I am not a religious person, rather I am a skeptic-materialist, but I have to confess that for the first time in my life I was begging God for help. I didn't know to which particular God my prayers were addressed—most likely to all of them, but I prayed furiously.

It seemed like an eternity passed while I crawled several yards and stopped the car just near the rock on the other side of the road. We were safe. Only then I felt that my legs and arms were wildly trembling. I shut off the engine and leaned on the back of my seat. It took some time before I was able to drive again. At the moment when I shut off the engine Susanna woke up. "What is the matter?" She wondered half asleep, "Why did we stop?"

My voice was a little hoarse, "Nothing, I just need to rest for a couple of minutes." I didn't tell Susanna what happened to us on that damned road. Being only half-awake she noticed nothing. It was still and quiet around.

Any Soviet long-distance driver faced many serious problems; and two of them caused special headaches: where to sleep and what to do if the car had a problem. These two problems were constant companions of all drivers. Car repair shops were even more infrequent than auto stores. I can't recall seeing at that time any gas station with a repair shop. For that reason my experience when the car cooling system fan unexpectedly broke during one of our trips is still in my memory.

We were driving on a highway with good speed when we heard a loud striking sound under the hood. After stopping the car and lifting the hood I found that one blade of the plastic cooling fan totally broke off close to its base. Knowing about the severe spare part shortage, when preparing for long trips I usually kept some certain parts in my car, but of course, not all. Nobody had complained before about a fan problem, and it had never come to my mind that the cooling fan could break.

The fan broke off in the early morning, and the morning coolness allowed me to not interrupt our trip. In such a condition I drove for over 500 kilometers making stops in many places to cool down the engine before finally I found a shop where a mechanic had the necessary spare parts and I replaced the fan using some of his tools.

Many people in my situation wouldn't risk driving if it could cause the engine to be overheated above the limit. The broken fan didn't stop our trip. I knew exactly what to watch and what to do in order to not damage the car and the engine. My knowledge and experience didn't come in a day. I bought a used car and when I bought it, figuratively speaking, I had a vague understanding of where to look for the engine. We had such an expensive and poor auto service that the word "poor" sounds more like a compliment. However, not too many car owners could do repair work themselves. I was among those who professed the "philosophy of independence"—I would take care of the car by myself as much as possible. Many people had a hard time when something went wrong with their car. They especially became helpless during journeys. Apparently it was the main reason why most women in the Soviet Union avoided driving cars. I don't remember ever seeing a woman driver on our numerous auto trips.

On one of our trips we were staying in a car camp near the North Caucasian city of Kislovodsk. We arrived in the evening, and a driver who was having trouble with his car drew my attention. Periodically, he was diving under the hood and then, returning, was looking around helplessly. I asked him what was wrong with the car. He immediately brightened and explained to me his problem. Fortunately, it wasn't a serious problem and I was able to help him. The word spread immediately. In the morning of the next day several drivers were waiting for me near our tent. For the three days that we were staying in the camp, drivers kept coming and asking for help. A sense of solidarity didn't allow me to refuse them and all three days they kept me busy with their cars.

When I described my business trip problems, I already mentioned my "pleasant" memories about the hotel ordeals. We experienced the same ordeals traveling by car. The problem of finding a place to stay overnight was a constant one for any traveler, and we weren't an exception. It caused us hours of worry and tons of nerves, though there were moments of luck.

I remember we couldn't find a place to stay one night in Kiev and came to the Kiev Tourist Camp late in the evening. Surprise, surprise: they had nothing available. We had exhausted all our options; the tourist camp was our last resort and we were going to sleep on the street—as always Susanna and children in the car, and I would have the pleasure of the open air. As we made our way to the door, the receptionist, a young woman, looked at us and said, "Where are you going? Listen, I live not far away from here in a one-room apartment. I'll be here the whole night. Would you like stay the night in my apartment?" It was already night outside; the children were as sleepy as winter flies, and we accepted the offer as a gift from God. She went with us to show us her apartment. We offered to pay but she refused to take the money. The next morning she came after her duty at the camp and treated us with tea. One could say that it wasn't a big deal but good things have a long memory regardless of how small they are.

We had a funny experience, again with an overnight stay, when we were in Lithuania. The night caught up with us driving through a village. After a long hard day, we were tired and exhausted, especially the children, and desperately needed a rest. More than once I heard from different people that Lithuanians didn't treat Russians in a friendly manner. Besides, it was common in many places for villagers to become suspicious when they saw strangers.

It was pitch-dark on the streets, not a living soul around, nobody to ask for advice or directions. Having no other choice we selected at random a couple of houses and asked their inhabitants for a shelter, just for one night or at least permission to stay near their houses. We had nothing to offer in return, except money. Alas, nobody wanted strangers even for pay. The situation seemed hopeless. We made one last attempt and unexpectedly were successful. Entering into a house we saw a family drinking tea. They seemed to have difficulty in understanding or maybe just pretended that they didn't know Russian. It is hard to tell how many times we repeated our request—for sure not once. Initially it was silence, then a man, who we understood to be a guest of the family, said, "Sure, you guys may stay in my house; we have plenty of available space. Let me show you my place."

He brought us to his house and told his wife that he had invited us to stay a night. It would have been fun to see how her facial expression changed, but we were too tired to pay attention. We offered money— she rejected it; we asked for an overnight stay only for the children— it didn't work either. The woman said that she was sorry but they had no place where they could accommodate us. Then she switched to Lithuanian, addressing only her husband. We couldn't understand a word, though it wasn't necessary to have an interpreter to understand what she was talking about. The husband, being embarrassed to look us in the eyes, began apologizing. The feeling was awful.

We were already near the porch when something moved in the woman's heart and she offered that we could sleep in their hayloft which was attached to the house and was a part of the cow-stall. For us, town-dwellers, the offer sounded a little unusual, nevertheless, we were glad: at least the children could have a safe rest. The night stay in the hayloft turned out to be a nice experience. Cows and other horned and hornless cattle respected our rest and didn't snore.

Someone said: "Anything is well that ends well." However, luck didn't always smile at us. On another occasion, we were returning from one of the Baltic republics. Our way home began in the morning, and after several hours of driving we were in the Belarus capital, the city of Minsk. There wasn't a chance for a hotel, and there was no point in wasting time in Minsk. On the other hand, it was early afternoon, and we decided to make a try in some smaller cities or towns. All tries were unsuccessful and I kept driving, hoping that maybe the next attempt would be better.

It was already dark before I understood the uselessness of any further attempts. According to the map we were within an hour from Kishinev and could make the overnight stop there with the Susanna's relatives. While we discussed the possibility, counted and recounted driving time, we realized that it could be late. It could be even later because we had never driven to Kishinev from that direction and weren't sure how to find their house quickly. Besides, we felt uncomfortable not giving them advance warning about our overnight visit. The children, exhausted with the monotonous road, had fallen asleep on the back seat long ago. Susanna also was nodding off to sleep. Apparently, we were at the most three hours from Odessa. Considering all those things, I finally made up my mind to go to Odessa without stopping anywhere.

We came home late at night. In total, I drove for seventeen hours without rest. It was my personal record and I have never had a chance to break it. During our car trips we had to overcome a lot of troubles, and along with that we also experienced the great joy of journeys, interesting adventures and meetings, and such wonderfully novel experiences that encourages many people to leave their comfortable homes and go into the new, mysterious world.

Thirty-Six

The Piano "Irmler"

1976

I always wanted my children to learn music. My mother inherited from her parents a nice, old piano. The piano was manufactured in the nineteenth century (~1860s) by the well-known German firm "Irmler"—hopefully I didn't make a mistake in the name—and had a bronze sounding board. I don't remember all the details exactly, but I was told that the instrument was a rarity. As a matter of fact, because of its great value it was stolen during the war after our family was forced to leave Odessa. The city had already come under fire by the German bombers.

Later on, my cousin, who during World War II was serving in the Soviet Army, managed to find it. I don't remember whether he participated in the liberation of Odessa, but it seems to me my parents told me that along with the troops, he entered the city, and when he came to see what happened to our apartment, he found out that the piano was gone. One of our neighbors saw who took it. Incidentally, robbers looted not only the piano from the apartment but also many other things: we lost everything we had. My parents managed to save a document with the serial number of the instrument on it, and knowing the number, which served as proof of our ownership, my cousin was able to get it back.

When Dina was a schoolgirl, we tried to teach her how to play piano. Alas, she didn't show much enthusiasm and the instrument became just a piece of useless furniture. Nevertheless, we didn't consider selling it, hoping that some day Vova would want to play. When we exchanged apartments and moved from Sverdlova Street to Lieutenant Lane, we couldn't take the instrument with us. It was too large and couldn't get through the door of our new apartment. Besides, our new apartment was so small that the piano would take about half of a room. So we decided to sell it. It was the only property inherited from my parents; but despite its value, it appeared to be difficult to find a buyer.

The piano was large and heavy, most people lacked space, and transportation was expensive. It turned into a suitcase without a handle: it was hard to carry but it was difficult to leave it. Finally, we decided to donate the piano to a kindergarten. Thus, at the time we lived on Lieutenant Lane, we had already given the piano away and couldn't teach Vova to play it. Unfortunately, other alternatives were beyond our possibilities.

Thirty-Seven

Praise to Enthusiasts

Enthusiasts hold up the world; they make a difference. This truth becomes especially understandable when you see the results of their work. The Soviet schools usually considered such things as the arts, music, aesthetics, etc., which were mostly taught in elementary schools, as a lesser matter in children's education. For many children it meant no art education at all. But sometimes schools hired somebody who considered their work as the most important thing in the world. Such a person, a music teacher, worked in Vova's school. His name was Miron Isaakovich. He was a great fan of opera music and each year created a program and prepared the children to perform children's musical shows and operas on the school stage. He managed to involve many children in that activity, and one of them was Vova. To our joy Vova enjoyed his music classes very much.

The teacher and students used to do everything necessary for the performances. Kids, mostly by themselves or sometimes with their parents' help, made theatrical decorations and costumes. They performed roles and played music. The teacher himself composed the music for some shows.

The name of the performance that I remember was *The Dragonfly and Ant*. The basis for the libretto was a fable of the famous Russian fable-writer Krylov, and the musical had the same name as the fable. The teacher, himself, composed the music. The fable had an educational meaning: When hard times came, the hardworking Ant was rewarded for its diligence, and the lazy, light-minded Dragonfly was punished for its laziness.

Vova used to share his joy with me, but to be honest, when he asked Susanna and me to come to the performance I didn't expect too much. We had a real, unexpected pleasure. The music was nice, and the children sang and danced beautifully. Vova played his part with great ardor. I enjoyed seeing him; he was really wonderful. I watched the show and thought, "Enthusiasts and optimists are really the Atlases of the human spirit." We felt great gratitude towards his teacher for the wonderful job.

One more teacher-enthusiast played a positive role in Vova's school life. It was an instructor from the special children's technical center called the City Station of the Young Technicians. I taught Vova all kinds of technical skills that I knew and was able to do. He was always happy to help me with the car and home maintenance and repairs. Unfortunately, my experience and skills with radio and electronic devices was limited. There was a technical center in the city where children under instructors' supervision learned different handy works, including the design of simple radio sets and electronic devices. Following my advice, Vova began attending the radio section of the station. He gained good experience, which appeared to be useful in his future career.

When Dina was a child I didn't try to teach her any handy mechanical work and technical skills, and it was a mistake. It happened partially because she didn't show an interest in mechanical toys and games and partially because I was in the captivity of the prejudice that "girls play with dolls and boys play with cars." I spent a lot of time solving many mathematical problems with her and developing her math capability, but told her little about physical and technical problems. Actually, sometimes I played simple construction and design games with Dina and noticed that she played without great interest and would get tired soon. It discouraged me and I didn't try to turn her attention to the challenging technical problems and didn't make attempts to develop her spatial and technical imagination.

I realized my mistake for the first time when she began having some difficulty with the descriptive geometry. I recalled it again when many years later I saw her attempting to fix a tap in her house. By the way, I had fun when I tried to help her and she interrupted me by saying, "I'll do it myself, you can't." Now I am thinking about these oversights with a feeling of guilt. The only "pardon" I could have: she is good in math.

Following my belief, I concentrated my efforts in developing Vova's engineering skills. Once I explained to him some basics of creative thinking and demonstrated certain rules of the Inventive Theory by examples from simple inventions. He got interested in the theory, and after that I tried to educate him a little in the matter. He was a smart boy and good listener.

The Soviet central newspaper for children *Pionerskaya Pravda* organized a competition among children for better solutions to technical problems. Some problems appeared to be difficult even for adults. Vova took part in the competition and won the newspaper's award by submitting an interesting, non-trivial solution.

The Inventive Theory was also created and developed by enthusiasts. Enthusiasts hold up the world; they make a difference. This truth becomes especially understandable when you see the results of their work.

Vova after performance

Thirty-Eight

The Sea Dances

My hometown Odessa, the Southern Ukrainian city, is big seaport on Black Sea. For me, Odessa was always inseparably associated with the sea. In the days of my youth and later after the birth of my children, I used to spend many summer hours at numerous sea beaches. Warm water, nice sand, tender southern sun attracted many Odessians and many hungry for the sea and the sun visitors from all over the country. All of that took place before most city beaches became dirty and polluted below the safety limits.

I liked the sea but hardly anybody would consider me as a true sea lover. I liked acquiring a tan and swimming; I liked boating moderately but never enjoyed fishing. I wasn't a vegetarian and liked to eat fish soup and almost any kind of fish dishes, but the sight of fish gasping for breath and fluttering on the hook spoiled my mood and made me sick. Besides, the process of fishing itself bored me. A couple of times, some of my friends took me fishing, and after that limited experience I have lost even those few droplets of fishing enthusiasm I had.

Numerous sad and sometimes tragic situations and events in my memory are related to the sea. I witnessed a couple of them, but have no desire to recall it. The sea doesn't like stupid arrogant jokes and requires a serious attitude toward it. On the other hand, funny "sea" stories and comic situations often recur to my memory. One of them I remember since my senior school years.

After several chilly weeks, it was the first really sunny day and many people rushed to the city beaches. I was among a group of boys who decided to go to the sea after classes. We couldn't swim: there was surf and the water was cold, and when one of the boys incidentally met his girlfriend, we left them chatting and went for a little walk. The boy who met his girlfriend, wishing to show his bravery to her, undressed and plunged into the water at the moment when the highest surf wave was about to hit the coast.

We weren't far away when we heard his cry and hurried back. The picture that opened in front of our eyes was a complete mess. People were crowded near the water and were looking at somebody. The boy in the water was crying something, but, because of the surf noise and people's talking, nobody was able to hear and understand what he was crying.

The waves were high; the water was chilly and he was losing his strength fast, though he still didn't seem to be in serious danger. However, after people saw that there were a couple of moments when he could get out from the water and failed to do so, two or three big athletic men jumped into the water to help him. To our astonishment, he didn't want to leave the water, fiercely resisting rescuers' help. He was strangely dancing and biting the men that were trying to release his arms. Finally, they managed to pull him out of the water—he appeared to be naked and as blue as an eggplant. In vain, we tried to find his clothes. Somebody fished some out of the water and brought him one of his shoes and his cap with a stone inside it. Apparently, the rest was still in the water, but there were no volunteers willing to jump into it. His girlfriend sacrificed her headscarf; we also made some sacrifices to cover his blue buttocks, and laughing and joking took him home.

Later we learned what happened with the young hero in the water. His jump into the surf was so strong that he didn't notice that the water had washed away his pants. When he realized his situation, it was too late: his pants were gone. And it wasn't over yet: bad luck didn't come alone—it seemed the same wave washed away his clothes which he carelessly dropped too close to the water. Somebody, after listening to the story, sarcastically noticed: "If you want to show your bravery be careful—hold on to your pants."

Thirty-Nine

The More I Like Dogs

1973 to 1987

Often we don't think much about the passing of time, unless some sad or joyful event interrupts the habitual flow of our life. We wished to bring a loyal friend and companion to Dina's life; we wished for a creature that would need her attention and care and would teach her to be responsible for another's well-being. That small puppy dog who we adopted required our complete attention, and sometimes even more than each of us. Adopting him, we didn't even remotely realize what a commitment it was necessary to make.

In my youth I was a cat lover. Living in Siberia we had a male cat. He loved to sleep on my neck and in my bed, play with me, and also spend much time with female cats, coming home wounded and without pieces of fur. Finally, this dissolute womanizer rewarded me with ringworm, and Mother had to treat us both.

Our second cat lived with us for a while when we came to Odessa. He was more moderate but had a habit of vanishing periodically.

Despite the mentioned troubles, cats need much less care than dogs and have a different personality; they are too independent and not so loyal. Cats could leave and never bother to say good-bye.

Tvel lived with us for fourteen years, up to his death. He developed habits which were changing with years. Some of his habits were funny, and some caused us worry and trouble. For a while, he liked to sleep in an armoire wrapping himself in blankets and sheets that we used to keep there. When he did it the first time, we couldn't find him and worried that somehow he managed to run away. We called and looked for him for more than an hour, turning all rooms upside down. It was unbelievable to find him in the wardrobe, because the wardrobe's doors were closed all the time. In the morning, while we were covering the sofa-bed he had managed in seconds to slip into it unnoticed. Nobody was able to guess where to look for him.

In the evening, he would sleep on the sofa-bed and get mad when Mom or Susanna tried to sit down next to him. He threateningly growled when he heard somebody opening the wardrobe door because he knew it was a signal that we would ask him to get off the sofa.

His visits to a veterinary clinic were exclusively my responsibility. Only I could hold him still. Sometimes thick gloves were necessary to protect my hands from his bites while the vet performed examinations or procedures. All vets were patient and kind, but scared Tvel fiercely bit everybody. Regardless of how we got to the vet clinic, by car or just walking, several blocks before it he began trembling and tried to hide or to go back. He had an incredible intuition, always unmistakably recognizing where we were going.

At the beginning, after Vova was born and we brought him home, Tvel was so visibly jealous of Vova that one could see him suffering every time we took care of the child. It was funny to see Tvel's big sad eyes and observe his behavior—fun for us but certainly not for him. He would run away, didn't want to eat, and was always hiding under the furniture. He understood that now Vova became the epicenter of the family. It took him a while to comprehend the family's hierarchy, accept the new priorities and make some adjustments. He still treated Dina as a "sister," but as an older "sister," and Vova, in his eyes, was a younger "brother." As an older brother he assumed his rights for priority and more respect. When Vova grew up a little, Tvel tried to show him his place: If Vova did something he didn't like, he chased Vova and barked at him. Once I came home and found a picture: Tvel and Vova, standing on all fours, face to face, were barking at each other.

Vova began to show his concern about Tvel at an early age. He was two when we asked him to take care of Tvel, to walk with him in the back yard and give him water and food. Following his angry nature, Tvel often wasn't "polite" with his "younger brother," but Vova patiently continued his duty and succeeded. Lasting kindness and sincere care finally gave birth to love and loyalty. As a gesture of the highest devotion, Tvel sometimes graciously allowed Vova to put a leash on his neck. He became Vova's best friend and loyal defender, fiercely attacking anybody to protect his "brother." And I have to say not only his brother. He was fearless protecting all members of our family. The spirit of a gladiator lived in his tiny body.

Tvel's initial attitude toward other animals was mainly based on their size. Small pets evoked if not his friendliness, then at least curiosity or a wish to become acquainted. He didn't fear big dogs, and meeting them he growled a warning or, just in a case, barked. By this all his appearance was saying, "You better take me seriously. Don't even think of touching me or my master." Not all dogs followed his warnings and once he became a victim of his assertiveness. He carelessly scolded a female bulldog, and she, irritated by his impoliteness, crushed him down by jumping on him. Fortunately, she was generous enough not to bite him but the psychological trauma was so deep that for over a month our hero was depressed and refused to go outside.

His experience with other representatives of the pet world also wasn't always happy. I still remember one of his attempts to strike up an acquaintance with a young lady. She was a sky-blue-eyed beauty with blond, soft hair. Without any false modesty, he considered himself a handsome male with a slender waist and broad chest. Several times he walked by but pretending that he was not paying much attention to her full of curiosity inviting looks. Finally he noticed her and went to that beautiful stranger to show his friendliness and a wish to get acquainted. He stretched out his neck not meaning anything inappropriate. At the moment he approached her he felt a slap on the face. The poor guy howled jumping back, not from pain—the slap was soft and shouldn't have caused any harm—but from the suddenness, lack of trust, and insult. He would never expect such guile. Since then our unfortunate "romantic" avoided all cats even if they looked nice and friendly.

Tvel affected our lives in many ways by bringing a lot of fun and joy and at the same time, more worry, care, and attention. Generally, he was a healthy dog. We tried to feed him with the same food we ate, but soon he refused to eat it, with the exception of meat. And he accepted not just any meat, but only quality meat. I have already had a chance to explain our problems with food: there was a shortage of regular food for people, and meat was in particularly short supply. Sometimes we managed to get so-called "Doctor" sausages and were happy with such luck. I don't know for sure what ingredients those sausages contained, but Tvel wasn't so happy; he didn't want to eat it. Apparently he felt that there was too much starch or cellulose in them. Frequently, I was forced to sacrifice my portion of meat for him. Any time when Susanna had a chance, she treated him with a piece of raw meat; alas, the holidays weren't often.

After a while, he began suffering from beriberi (avitaminosis). The Soviet food industry didn't produce food for pets. The poor animal needed a well-balanced diet, but we had no way to get it. When I tried to put even a tiny vitamin pill in his food, Tvel carefully ate everything around the vitamin, leaving the pill untouched. The only remedy I invented was to chew a piece of meat and mix it with chewed vitamins or grass. (I didn't chew the grass—I just couldn't do it.) It is necessary to admit that my inventiveness wasn't much help; I didn't know which vitamins and minerals to use and how much was necessary to add. As our acquaintance, a veterinary professor, told us, "You created a human life for him and he got human problems."

Later on, we used different tricks to force him to eat vitamins. I used to prepare the mixture with food, grass, and vitamins, and, making a grabbing gesture, I would say, "I will take it away." He became angry, barked and ate the mixture. Unfortunately, it didn't work every time. There were moments when he would smell his dish and silently run away from it. He would look at me, his big black eyes would become sad and, it seemed, he was saying, "Try it yourself, I'll see how you would like it." It was hard to feed a skeptical, politically ignorant dog with slogans about abundance...

Fleas were the second huge problem. At times, it seemed, he had more fleas than hairs. Whatever we tried to get rid of this disastrous insects' invasion just didn't work. Our vet pharmacies could offer only some special chemicals, and those chemicals could kill a dog along with the fleas. Once after we used them, Tvel, inhaling their vapors, lost consciousness. We panicked, not knowing what to do and where to go for help; it was late evening and the vet clinic had been closed long ago. Suddenly it dawned upon Susanna to try sea air. We rushed him to the beach for fresh sea air. Because of that, or regardless, he gradually regained his consciousness. The next day the doggy was pretty much alive. Fortunately, he survived without any consequences but I am sorry to say—the fleas survived as well.

The most trouble we had with Tvel was during our car travels. We had no dog hotels or shelters. There wasn't anybody to take care of him even for a day or two, not to mention two or three weeks. So, we had no choice other than to take the dog with us on all family trips. It made it an unforgettable experience. I have already written that at that time it was a tremendous problem in most cases to find a hotel either in a big or small city, practically anywhere. But even if luck smiled upon us and we managed to get a room, nobody would allow us to bring in the dog. We had to bring him in secretly, preliminarily lulling the administration's vigilance. I think Tvel clearly understood it. When putting him in a zipped bag, we smuggled him into the room; that usually noisy monster was as silent as a sleepy fish.

A couple of times we tried to leave him in the room during the day and go somewhere. Coming back, we found ourselves in big trouble: Tvel revealed his presence, protecting our room and property from strangers. Hotel residents passed by or a housemaid wanted to clean the room, his doggy nature prevailed, and he was getting hysterical, disclosing our "big secret."

Because of him, excursion tours became a forbidden fruit. Guides usually didn't allow us to take him with us. Thus, one of us, Susanna or I, used to go on an excursion with the kids, leaving the other one with Tvel. It was the same situation with cafes and restaurants. Only once, in Estonia, a woman guide, filled with sympathy for him, allowed us all, including Tvel, to participate in the bus tour. We couldn't leave him in our car for long because it was too hot and dangerous for him.

So, he was with us everywhere we went, and it wasn't always a pleasant experience for him. I recall when we were traveling in the Caucasus, we made a stop in the city of Pyatigorsk. The weather was extremely hot. We hardly could tolerate it, and Tvel suffered the most. The poor guy couldn't walk, and we carried him, looking for shade and stopping every fifteen minutes to give him some water. To see the city sights we took a city bus. The bus was overcrowded and packed like sardines, and on top of everything, it was incredibly hot inside. Tvel gave up completely; we thought he was dying. People sympathized with him and made some room around us so we were able to wet his head and give him a drink. I recall many other, maybe not so dramatic, similar situations. They were hard, but there was some good side to it— the way we treated the situations was a good lesson of care, responsibility, and humanity for our children.

Tvel began living with us in 1973. Vets say that to compare the dog's age with people's it is necessary to multiply its actual age by seven. If we are to believe these calculations, in 1987 Tvel was about 100 years old. We saw him aging. He went gray and gradually turned from an energetic and aggressive young monster into an old, wise, philosophically calm thinker. Now we didn't worry that all of a sudden he would chase a cat or a dog, or run somewhere, and we trusted him. We could even leave him alone in the backyard. Like an old man, he used to get out of the house into the yard and would sit and squint from the bright sun. Vova still took good care of his old friend, and did it with more respect for his solid age.

One day we noticed that Tvel wasn't his usual self. He was moaning all night. Several times during the night we woke up and approached him but couldn't find what was wrong with the dog. Early in the morning I rushed him to the vet clinic. The veterinarian examined him carefully and said that his heart was weak. He gave him an injection. Sometimes it seemed that the dog was getting a little better, but the next night was also sleepless for us. By the morning he calmed down. In the middle of the day Tvel silently died. We all weren't ashamed to cry.

With Vova's help I buried him at the coastal park, not far away from our home. After a while, someone presented me with several young oak trees. I, together with Vova, planted one of them in the place where we buried Tvel. He was a loyal and smart dog. Sometimes I was thinking with astonishment, "How is it possible, in such a fist-sized head, for there to be so much understanding and brain?" Tvel was a pet, but he wasn't just a piece of fur with two ears and four legs. Although we had many troubles with him, he brought a lot of joy and many other wonderful feelings into our family. His death gave rise to some of my joyless thoughts about human nature, in general, and what we saw around us, in particular.

It was painful to observe the constant degradation of the human qualities in the society we lived in. Decades of the hypocrisy of the government policy, double moral standards and double standards in people's treatment, shameless lies and suppression, and physical extermination of political or ideological causes were still fresh in the memory of many people. All of that had destroyed many human feelings in people's souls. Again and again came to my mind the words of the famous Czech writer Carel Capek saying "The more I learn about people the more I like dogs."

Forty

Apartment Exchange

1976 to 1977

When Susanna's mother got seriously ill, it was a warning call for us. Her parents needed constant daily help and care and we realized that if we continued to live far away from them we wouldn't be able to help. We had begun our first attempts to make an exchange of their and our rooms in communal apartments for one larger apartment in order to live together. In our situation, considering what we were offering for the exchange, it was "mission impossible." Our rooms were in communal apartments, and the facilities were shared with other families. We were tired of living in such apartments in the conditions we had lived almost our entire life. Our dream was to get a separate apartment only for our parents and us.

Those who have had a lifelong dream know how hard it is to part with your dream. We got sick and tired of living in an overpopulated communal apartment, and we felt it especially keenly after realizing that along with Susanna's father's tragic death our last hope died. Although nothing changed in our communal routine, the lines to the toilet and to the bathroom, which was separate from the toilet, became intolerable. Converted from a small corridor, our "nice" kitchen that we were sharing with three other families was a little too "tight in the thighs." It was so small that, when four people were preparing their food at the same time, they couldn't avoid touching each other. We lived in communal apartments our whole lives, dreaming about privacy. Now we became obsessed with that thought and despite the helplessness of our situation decided to look for an exchange again.

For a long time we couldn't find anything suitable to exchange for our two communal rooms. Unexpectedly such an opportunity appeared after our neighbor mentioned that his sister who had a small, separate apartment wouldn't mind exchanging it for our larger room. Thus, we could offer the separate apartment and one communal room. Using that combination, we found a separate, but, to put it mildly, not very nice apartment. The apartment was as tiny as a ship cabin and had many other disadvantages. Despite that we were happy: at last, we had a separate apartment and didn't have to share it with strange families. No more long lines to the toilet or to the bathroom in the morning and a kitchen where we could be without neighbors. Such luxury was hard to imagine. The apartment was situated in a small two-story residential building.

It was a stone building over a hundred years old that was located on small street, quiet in wintertime and overcrowded in summer. That part of the city was a typical old Odessa neighborhood with some colorful people living in it. It became an interesting experience and an unforgettable part of our lives.

The apartment was on the ground floor. Apparently, it was once a three-room apartment which later had been divided between two families. One of the families got a room without facilities although with the entrance through the front door. We "inherited" an entrance into our apartment through the kitchen, but it wasn't the only disadvantage. The worst part about the entrance was its extreme inconvenience and a terrible sight of a slum. The entrance door was under a rusty metal staircase, which led to the second-floor apartments. Because of that, the door was shorter than a standard door and in order to get into the apartment it was necessary even for a person of average height to bend down, otherwise bumps or bruises on the head were inescapable. A couple of our first-time visitors, who were too "grand" to bend, were punished for their "overconfidence." The entrance created quite an ugly impression, and my first project was to transfer the entrance to another wall.

The apartment had two separate rooms, approximately 200 square feet and 120 square feet. A partition divided the larger room into two parts. Later on, I installed a door to separate the smaller part from the larger one and thus, created a tiny, narrow and gaunt (approximately five-foot by twelve-foot) "room." The only convenience of that "room," which I proudly called "my study," was that I could work in it as late as I needed without disturbing the rest of the family. The study was so tiny that it barely had space for a desk, a chair and bookshelves along the wall. During the previous twenty years I had collected a personal library with many scientific, technical, fictional, art, and other books (I believe 1,500 to 2,000 books). The apartment had an individual radiator heating system, a gas stove, and later on, we installed a gas water heater so that the family could enjoy a hot shower or a bath.

The capacity of telephone station in Odessa was extremely limited and that created an unsolvable problem with telephone installation. Ordinary people could be on a waiting list over twenty years and sometimes a lifetime. We had a communal telephone in our previous apartment. Our new apartment had no telephone, and we never were able to get a new one, although when we emigrated we were on the waiting list over ten years. Almost twenty years ago we emigrated from the Soviet Union, and I am afraid we still are on the waiting list...

In addition to the apartment, we "inherited" two sheds from the previous residents. One of them was a so-called "summer room" converted from the larger shed. Our inheritance also included two grape vines and a tiny area with plants next to our windows which faced the backyard. Later on, I managed to use that area as a parking place for my car. Therefore, with the exception of the telephone, we almost managed to live as the rest of the civilized world.

In a certain way our new place did have some indisputable advantages. One of them was great location, which, in my judgment, was the best in the city. It combined several features that rarely come together in one location of a big city. We lived in a resort area approximately 200 meters above sea level and enjoyed beautiful sea air. There were no urban pollutants from industry or big streets with many cars. Our building was situated a couple of hundred meters from one of the best Odessa sea beaches. The district had a nice, poetic name, "Otrada," associated in our minds with joyful feelings, with pleasure and delight.

At night we could hear the sounds of the surf and the other voices of the sea. It took no more than five to seven minutes to walk to the beach. Our tiny, 100-yard-long street was transformed into a small road closer to the beach. It rolled down toward the sea through a coastal shady park with many trees and bushes. A convenient passenger cableway was built above the park between the residential area and the beach. The sea was so close to our house that we didn't even bother to dress fully and often walked to the beach in our swimsuits. After work, almost every summer weekday whenever I had any chance or during weekends and during vacation time, I used to take Dina and Vova to the Otrada coast, and we would spend hours on the beach.

The other advantage of the location was its closeness to our jobs, just a ten-minute walk. It was also close to public transportation (streetcar and trolleybus) stops, to the main railroad terminal, to the famous city main market, called "Privoz" (English approximate translation of the word is "Food supply"), to many big shops, and to some other important places. Indeed, it was a great location. Now when I hear the American realtors' famous slogan, "Location, location, location," it always makes me recall our former residence.

Having such advantages and living in a separate apartment, it was no wonder that we enjoyed our new place. Unfortunately, there was the other side of the coin; the apartment required a lot of different improvements and repairs. I have to add that they were endless. I was doing them as long as we lived there, learning many things, like plumbing, carpentry, plastering, and numerous other types of repairs. The Russian optimists would love to say: "There is no bad without something good" (The American equivalent—"Every cloud has a silver lining"). Recalling our "epic" with the apartment exchange, I could say many things about our new dwelling, both good and bad; however, we did not feel it was a big inconvenience in living like sardines. There was something bigger.

The inventory of apartments in Odessa was extremely poor though it was common for the whole country. Our choices were even more limited since communal apartments were undesirable, and it required great luck to find something acceptable and suitable. People desperately were trying to improve their living conditions, and frequently it was just not possible. I don't know what some of them expected when they described in their ads that they were ready to exchange a palace for an ordinary apartment. For that reason, each ad had to be checked thoroughly. What sounded extremely attractive in an advertisement could be just the opposite in reality, and sometimes, it became comical.

Once we read in an advertisement book for apartment exchange about a tempting offer. Judging from the advertisement, the offer had many advantages: It was exactly what we were looking for. Not wasting any time for discussions, Susanna and I rushed to see that promising offer.

The rooms were ordinary, and at the end of the visit, I asked if we could see the bathroom and other facilities as well. The woman guided us back to one of the rooms in the middle of which was a table with a couple of chairs. The scene was typical for any traditional living or dining room. Then something stunning happened. The woman moved the table away, and we saw that under it was something covered with a blanket. With the gesture of a circus magician, she pulled away the blanket and what we saw shocked even my wild imagination. Under the blanket, like monument of Human Creativity stood... a white toilet bowl.

It took a while for me to come to my senses. Then I asked, "How are you supposed to use it?"

"Just move the table away and do what you need to do," the woman explained seriously, and I painted a picture in my mind. Susanna and I silently looked at each other. With all my strength I was fighting to keep a straight face. One would think that it was a joke. But it wasn't.

Forty-One

My Stories

1988

I liked literature and read a lot. Sometimes I also felt a thirst to write. While in high school, I tried to write short poems. They were mostly fables, an imitation of the famous Russian fable-writer Krylov. Later on, when I was a college student and even after graduation, I tried to write short stories. The topics of some of them I still remember. Just as an example of what excited me and occupied my mind, I would like to mention the subjects a couple of my stories.

One story was about a young pianist. His piano teacher frequently told him that his playing sounded too cold and lacked emotion. Preparing for a performance at his forthcoming piano concert, the pianist tried hard. But the teacher still wasn't satisfied at the lack of emotions in his performance.

Just before the concert, the young man quarreled with his girlfriend and became upset. At the concert he played Beethoven's Moonlight Sonata. While playing, he thought of his girlfriend, how he loved her, and how he was afraid that they would break up. He played with much feeling. Actually, he didn't play; he simply described how he felt. When he finished, the audience was delighted. His teacher was overwhelmed...

By the way, the story had a prototype. I knew a piano player who inspired me to write that story. She would play Beethoven or Chopin unemotionally, cold as a fish, and as I listened to her and thought, "My goodness, has she ever fallen in love with anybody?"

The other story was about love, which didn't stand the test of even a short separation. There were more short stories about friendship, a dog's loyalty, and other things. I can't judge my compositions. Maybe they were naïve and childish. It didn't matter. I was writing just for myself, for self-expression. I believe it was nothing serious or worthwhile. Maybe sometimes I felt the necessity to put down my thoughts or something else—it is hard to tell. I didn't show the stories to anybody and never had even the slightest intention to publish any of my "literary exercises"; I just wanted to save them for myself and kept the manuscripts in my personal archive. Sometimes it is useful to look inside myself.

I don't know after whom I inherited my bent for writing, because neither my father nor my mother ever showed an inclination to write anything, besides letters and business papers. But my children apparently inherited the taste for writing from me. When Dina and Vova were small kids, they used to write "novels" and verses. I managed to save some of them and still keep Dina's "opus" and a couple of Vova's "novels" and verses in my now quite skinny American archive. As far as I know, unlike me, they seem to have "outgrown" that childhood passion.

Shortly before our emigration from the USSR, I was told that the authorities wouldn't allow us to take our personal papers, including any kind of manuscripts. Whether it was the spy mania or designed to simply humiliate us, or both, I don't know, and it didn't make a big difference. My main fear was that the papers would be confiscated, and our journey would be halted at the border.

Indeed, such incidents took place. We didn't want to take any chances, and I certainly didn't want my archive to fall into the wrong hands. Besides my "literary exercises," I kept many personal things in my archive, like letters, poems, some photos with inscriptions, etc., which no matter what, I didn't wish to be taken or read by anybody else. Knowing that it would be impossible to take my archive with me, I burned it with the exception of several items which I didn't have the guts to annihilate. I hid those items in clothes and managed to take them out with me. I burned the rest. When I was burning my papers, I felt that along with my archive I burned a part of my memory, a part of my life…

Solomon
There is a lot to think about

Forty-Two

The Neighbors

We were in the preparation stage to leave the country. After getting our exit visas, we were ready to say goodbye to our relatives, friends, and neighbors. Before we told them, some neighbors had learned about our emigration from a passport clerk to whom we handed over our passports as part of the citizenship withdrawal procedure. It was an open secret that all passport clerks were snitches ("Stukach" as people called them in Russia), in other words, police and KGB informers. In any case, we weren't going to leave without saying goodbye to our former neighbors.

Usually we lived in good neighborhoods close to the city downtown. But there were several other locations which were popular in Odessa and desirable for many people. We used to live in one of them. Many "VIPs" loved to get dwellings in that neighborhood. Judges, generals, regional party bosses and other former and current "big potatoes" populated the area. However, when we moved in, we found out that the small area that was populated by our immediate neighbors (I mean those who lived in our building, or to be more accurate, in our yard) was kind of a "preserve" or an "island." In outward appearance, they were mostly ordinary, low-working-class people.

They were the most "intellectual" people in the yard: husband, wife and their daughter. The husband was a retired admin clerk and a member of the Communist Party. His daughter graduated from a college. Apparently, because of their "higher" social status, they had limited contacts with most neighbors and kept them at an arm's length.

A retired worker occupied the other part of the building with his wife, daughter, son-in-law, and their son. The wife suffered from an illness that caused her deadly complications. Their son-in-law was a heavy alcoholic. Soon after we moved in, being dead drunk, he broke both his legs and couldn't go anywhere. His family settled him in their garage because he couldn't use the stairs. They refused to supply him with vodka, hoping to break his heavy addiction. But their efforts remained in vain; he couldn't stand life without a daily portion of alcohol and one night he committed suicide by stabbing himself to death with a kitchen knife. After a while, his wife got married again and moved to her husband's apartment.

It wasn't the only family with alcoholic problems. There was another family with similar problems, and again, the problems were with the younger generation. They lived with the wife's parents. It was a retired elderly couple, a husband, a simple and a good-natured man, his wife, and their daughter with her husband and their son. Having only two small rooms in a communal apartment for the whole family, they had converted their shed into a dwelling and the older couple lived there. He died several years before our emigration.

A family of three lived not far away from us: mother, (rarely did anyone call her by her given name) her daughter, and her daughter's son. Without exaggeration, they were like a special species in our neighborhood and maybe even the city.

It was the most scandalous family in our yard, possibly in the whole region. Especially distinguished was the daughter. Her "elegant" lexicon consisted primarily of untranslatable words and expressions that made some nervous intellectuals with too sensitive an ear lose their consciousness after hearing just a couple of her linguistic samples. Actually, she was a bilingual lady; obscene words were her main language and sometimes she put in her speech a limited number of Russian words which served as links.

As a rule, she communicated with people using just three words: "f… your mother." Anyone who tried to make a literal interpretation of the expression would be absolutely wrong. In her lexicon, the expression had a range of different meanings. Depending on intonation, these three words could mean anything from amazement and delight to anger and sorrow. Even her mother, who wasn't much different from her and was familiar with her daughter's rich vocabulary, sometimes, hearing some of her pearls, became speechless and petrified with an open mouth.

The daughter had one more nickname commonly used in such situations: the "Black Mouth," which in Russian was equivalent to the American "Dirty Mouth." Her most favorite and most exquisite expression one could translate as: "Don't make a bullet from a penis." The last word of this impressive phrase she pronounced with great enthusiasm and pleasure. Again, the expression had many meanings depending on the context. It could mean, "You exaggerate," or "don't tell me lies," or "don't try to look better than you are," and could have many other meanings as well. I have to admit that my linguistic education wasn't enough to know and understand fully her rich vocabulary.

Her appearance corresponded to her lexicon; she resembled a witch that illustrators liked to draw in Russian children's books. Her mouth was so big that it didn't leave room for a brain. When she was in a good mood, her best dream, which she would share with some neighbors, was to have "a bottle of vodka and a big male in her bed." While saying that, she would roll up her eyes, lustfully smiling.

In addition to her extremely vulgar and scandalous character, she was a primitive man-hater. I use the word "primitive," because she was primitive herself. She had no idea what she was talking about. When she learned that we were going to emigrate she was shouting, "You Jews are always take advantage of us. You are leaving us to rot here." Actually, she wasn't a "pure" anti-Semite; she was anti-everybody and anti-everything, just full of blind hatred. All the neighbors avoided communicating with her, breathing with relief if she passed by without comments.

The next family I would like to mention was a family of five: two couples—an older couple and a younger one and their son. All adults in the family were drinkers. They always needed money for vodka, and the daughter used to borrow money from Susanna a couple of times a month and then had a hard time returning the money.

Sometimes, for unknown "drunken" reasons, the older man and his son-in-law fought with each other. During one such fight, the father stabbed the son-in-law with a kitchen knife. Fortunately, the injury wasn't fatal. I have to add that in my memory, nobody ever called the police in any yard conflicts and fights regardless of how serious they were.

Often, the father drank with another neighbor. They had a strange love-hate relationship—before drinking they were friends, after finishing a bottle of wine or vodka they usually rushed to fight. At times, it was a cruel fight with metal rods and bricks. Sometimes their friend and occasional "negotiator" made risky attempts to stop them, but it was in vain: the fighters were too much into it.

I would like to mention about one more neighbor. He, his wife, daughter, and son lived in a dumpy basement apartment. They were decent and hardworking people; their living conditions were worse than poor, and for many years the family was desperately trying to get a better apartment. The son suffered from a horrible disease at a young age. I don't remember the name of the disease; it was a kind of progressive bone liquefaction, which caused slow paralysis of the whole body. It was painful to see how his disease gradually disabled him. When, finally, they got the apartment, the boy could hardly walk.

Vova sympathized with him. When we came to America and Vova earned his first few dollars, the first thing he did was send a present to the boy. It was a digital watch with several convenient features. After a while we got the package back with the postal notice that the watch had disappeared. It got lost or stolen. Who knows? The post office failed to explain. It was a mystery, a disappointing mystery, especially for Vova. So, he bought a new watch and sent it again. Fortunately, this time it arrived without unwanted surprises.

I still remember my feelings when after the exchange we moved to our new apartment. At first I felt like "rara avis" (a rare bird, in Russian it sounds like "a white crow"). Soon we established friendly relationships with most of the neighbors. They saw that despite my white-collar job, I wasn't afraid of physical work like maintaining my car, doing repairs and many other things with my hands, and that all was well respected and appreciated. I wasn't ashamed to ask things I didn't know, and they willingly showed or explained to me everything I needed, even lending their tools. Some of our neighbors invited us to join their parties where they, according to a Russian tradition, used to drink full eight-ounce glasses of vodka, but, knowing my drinking ability, poured a small drink in a glass for me, delicately asking if it was enough. I don't know how to explain that phenomenon—we weren't friends, but they had sincere respect for me.

The day of departure was fast approaching and we were short on time; nevertheless, the day before our departure I visited all of our neighbors. Their reaction to our emigration differed. Some of them said that they wished they could do the same. For most of them saying good-bye was sad. Women's eyes got wet. They hugged me and I felt that they restrained themselves from crying. The reaction from one of them surprised and touched me. When I came and told her that we were leaving, she hugged and kissed me and, being unable to control her tears, began crying as if we were close relatives.

They were simple people, and their life was hard, but often their hearts were kind. And regardless of how hard your life is, regardless of what you expect in your future, it is always difficult to part with those who for many years were respectful and kind to you, who were your good neighbors, and who understood your situation much better than many others. When parting forever, you begin to understand that one of the most valuable parts of human life is human ties.

Almost twenty years after leaving the country, I was able to make a short trip to Odessa and visit the yard hoping to see anybody from our past. What I learned made me believe in fate—I couldn't find anybody—their fate was tragic: almost all of the families had disappeared; the people died from unknown diseases, from alcoholism, and one was killed... New people populated the old yard; they were not able to tell me much information: they didn't know their predecessors.

Forty-Three

Language Has to Be Common

It was the third year of my life in America. I was on a streetcar in San Francisco and got into a conversation with a man. After numerous questions like "What?" "How?" "Why?" my new acquaintance said to me: "You have a distinctive accent, unusual structure of phrase, and interesting word selection. I wonder what country you are from. By the way, where did you study English?

I laughed. "What a nice way to comment my language." I had never heard a more polite assessment of my modest English, but my fellow traveler's question made me recall how I got my second language and what it took me.

My relationship with the language has a long history. Both the teaching and studying of foreign languages in the Soviet Union—especially in the fifties and sixties—was, mildly speaking, formal and ineffective. Most Soviet people didn't know foreign languages. There wasn't any need or motivation to study them. Soviet people couldn't freely travel abroad; they had no access to the modern foreign literature, and even if somebody managed to find foreign newspapers or foreign books, they were mainly reprinted and censored issues of the communist press and were so boring that they could even make an insomniac sleepy.

The vast majority of the second-language teachers had limited knowledge of the languages they taught, and they had no possibility of improving through practice. Even those who knew the second language a little better, without practice, soon forgot it. It was a well-known embarrassing story (possibly not just one) when a group of Soviet teachers of English was invited to meet with a delegation of American teachers, the Soviet teachers weren't able to translate the speech of their American colleagues.

Students couldn't know less than many of their teachers only because there was no such thing as negative knowledge. They usually spoke little of the second language and most studied only formal grammar in isolation from the language as a whole, though there existed some exceptions for elite schools and special institutes. My English teacher was so impressed by the fact that the English (and also French) word "pigeon" in Russian slang meant a young dandy that it became the only topic we discussed the whole curriculum year, nothing else.

I was keen to learn English and tried to study it myself, at home, but unfortunately it was for a very short time. Although compared to many other students, I knew it better, by any standard it wasn't language.

Teaching second languages, colleges used an even more formal approach than elementary and secondary schools. Colleges planned hours for self-study of a foreign language. The test consisted in reading and translating technical texts. But there was a catch: I witnessed many cases when teachers didn't understand technical terms and students could translate whatever came in their minds. The scores depended on intonation: the more confident you sounded the higher your score.

In general, I had a wish to study English, but that good intention remained just an intention—I always felt a lack of time, then my daughter was born, then I was busy at my work, then something else. When I needed to read an article in a foreign language for my work, we had a translator. Finally, I forgot those couple of words I had managed to remember, never trying to learn the language seriously. That was a wrong decision, and thirty years later I understood the mistake I had made. It was when I made up my mind to leave the country.

During our preparation for emigration, the situation didn't allow for time to learn English. The prospect of having trouble or being fired from my job (in the Soviet Union, those who wanted to leave the country were treated as traitors) forced me to conceal our wish to emigrate. Nevertheless, English remained one of my priorities and after we got permission to leave the country I used every spare minute to learn the language.

To accelerate the process I needed some help. My wife knew English; she graduated from a three-year course, and I asked her for help. She suggested that I read a text for the very beginners to find out the level of my English and decide whether she could help. I looked into the text and was able to recognize only two words: "Yes" and "No.. I looked at my wife and had no need to ask her about her decision.

My son-in-law appeared to be more accommodating or, perhaps, he was being respectful of my gray hairs (being over fifty isn't the best age to start learning language). Silently he listened to my reading with a very sad face. He didn't refuse to help me, but his face became much sadder.

While preparing for our emigration, I lived under tremendous stress; my nervous system was utterly strained. As a result, I almost lost my memory; I forgot words before I had a chance to repeat them. I only had a short period of time to learn English and believed that my first priority in the language was to gain a proper vocabulary. For this purpose, I developed my approach.

I read a page with English text and marked all unknown words. Then I copied all of them and translated them with the help of an English-Russian dictionary. Then I selected what were, in my opinion, the most important and frequently repeated words and copied them into a special copybook. I repeated each word ten, a hundred, a thousand times trying to remember it.

Like hammering nails into a concrete wall, I hammered words in my brain, learning to use any spare minute, any available time, including morning jogging and toilet procedures. I continued to "hammer nails," they bent, but the wall gradually gave away. I developed some vocabulary and was able to ask simple questions without the use of a dictionary.

Soon learning English, with minor exceptions, became my priority and my main headache. It was a challenge for me and I kept repeating to myself, "I must do it whatever it takes." By all means I tried to diversify methods of learning, tactics, and approaches in order to find what would work best for me.

From the first day that we arrived at the refugee camp in Italy, I started looking for English classes. There was one school with several classes of different levels, and the starting-level class was for those whose knowledge of English was limited to the fact that such a language existed. There were several classes at higher levels, from the medium to high level, including the most advanced class, organized specifically for medical doctors for whom language was a matter of the highest priority. My philosophy was to enter a class which would be, at least, one level higher than my current level: the harder the material the better chance to learn more.

After a while I felt that I was "ripe" to take the next step; I wanted to attend the most advanced class. To attend this class everybody had to pass a test. The teacher usually asked rapidly, almost like a tongue twister: "Where are you from?" If you answered, she would ask more questions; if you didn't understand her mumbling, you failed the test. I understood what she said, but didn't understand what she meant: city, or country, or region, or something else. The teacher didn't waste time; her verdict was final. So, having no choice, I continued in the "old" class.

I also continued self-education using my "word by word" approach and paying attention to each single word. It was a real Sisyphean toil, slow, but I didn't see any other way. There were delays when I had unexpected difficulties with the translation, and once I got in an embarrassing situation.

The Soviet edition of the English-Russian dictionary that I used didn't have some American words. Once, reading an American book, I came across several words which were absent from my dictionary. This didn't happen often and didn't prevent me from understanding the overall meaning of the text. But there was a word that some characters repeated many times and yet, I wasn't able to guess what it meant. The word was printed fully, and according to English grammar and literary style could be a part of speech like a verb, adverb, or adjective, or something else. It ignited my curiosity.

No Russian experts whom I asked about the word could translate it. So, when I met one of our American teachers, a young lady, I didn't hesitate to ask for help. When I showed her the word she thickly blushed and said: "You don't need this word." The way she replied and her reddened face made me realize that something was wrong with my question. Yes, my guess was correct—it was the f-word. This time I blushed, apologizing for my ignorance and unintentional embarrassment. Nevertheless, the incident didn't stop me from asking questions.

Especially frustrating for me was the fact that at that time we didn't know where to hear English speech, where to watch TV in English, or where to find someone with whom to speak English. We couldn't afford tape recorders, and the radio was only in Italian, which I didn't even bother trying to study. There was a great irony that the beautiful, melodic Italian became a forbidden fruit. English had already exhausted my language-learning abilities. Scared that it could spoil my frail English, I was avoiding Italian.

I tried to read as much as possible, hoping that it would improve my vocabulary. I took a few books written in English with me; some of them were too simple, others too difficult and boring. I craved for something that had modern American vocabulary. After a long search in the main town library, which had only three books written in English, and among them I fished out the only suitable book, *On the Other Side of Midnight* by Sydney Sheldon. It was my first attempt to read a real American book that had not been adapted or simplified.

When I read the book for the first time, according to my established approach I marked each unknown, doubtful, or unintelligible word. On average, there were twenty to forty words per page. With time, my "productivity" increased, especially when Vova helped me. Sometimes he copied the words I had marked and translated them with the help of an English/Russian dictionary, saving me a lot of time. Finally, my sweaty "labor of Sisyphus" was rewarded. After a short while my vocabulary improved; I pretty well understood what I read and started to really enjoy my reading. When we walked with our friends, I was retelling them (of course, in Russian) chapters of Sheldon's book. They listened to me with great interest and each time asked to hear more.

I made progress but still there was a long way to go. I was going to live in a new country and desperately wanted to know the language. I wanted to have American friends, watch American TV and movies, and understand American culture. I became a "perpetual" student.

After living in America for a while I learned from my experience how it was important to know the language, how language united people, and how it contributed to better personal contacts. When people want to reach consent and mutual understanding they look for common language. It is a necessity. Language has to be common.

Printed in the United States
99525LV00002B/198/A